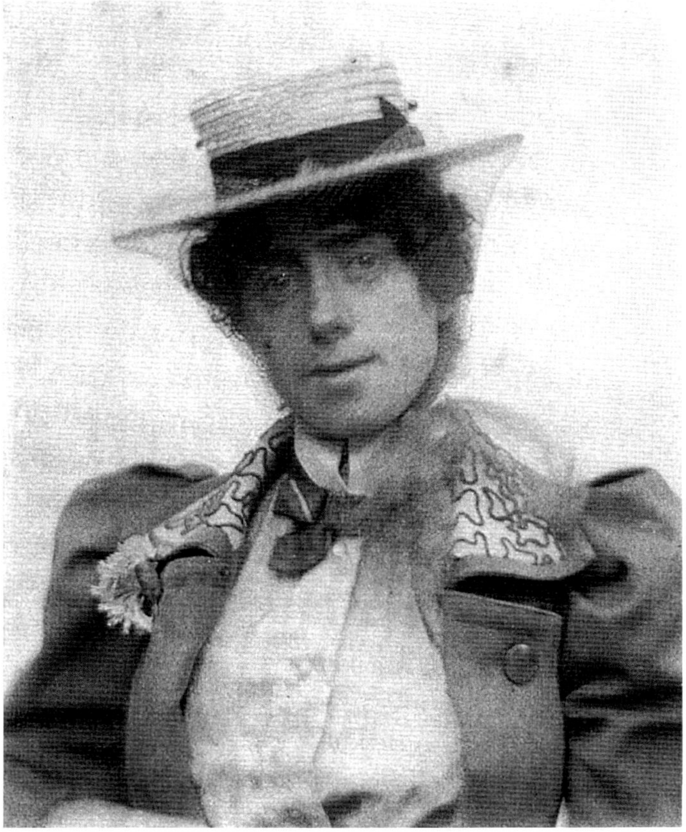

Bessie MacNicol

New Woman

AILSA TANNER

Privately published in Great Britain by the author 1998

ISBN 0 9533697 0 6

Designed and typeset in Garamond by Bill Smith
Production consultant Paul Harris
Printed in The Republic of Slovenia by Gorenjski Tisk

CONTENTS

Dimensions are expressed in inches (height x width)

ACKNOWLEDGEMENTS

As I have been involved with this book for over twenty years, there are several persons that I wish to acknowledge who unfortunately are no longer alive. I would like to record most gratefully the help I received from Libby Young, Joan and Bernard Dunn, Flora Hopkins, Jean Stewart Brown and George Bridges.

I have been greatly assisted by members of staff, past and present, of public collections and libraries in Scotland, who have been unfailingly helpful. I would like to thank in particular Helen Smailes of The National Galleries of Scotland, Anne Donald and Hugh Stevenson of Glasgow Art Gallery and Museum, Kelvingrove, Pamela Robertson and Martin Hopkinson of the Hunterian Art Gallery, University of Glasgow, and Liz Dent of the Lillie Art Gallery, Milngavie. I am indebted to the National Library of Scotland and the Mitchell Library in Glasgow for a great deal of assistance. I am especially grateful to Graham Hopner and Arthur Jones of Dumbarton Library for helping to trace the MacNicol family background. Thanks are also due to the Archives of both the University of Glasgow and Strathclyde University.

I would also like to express my thanks for permission to quote from the letters of Bessie MacNicol at Broughton House, Kirkcudbright, initially the property of the Hornel Trust and now of The National Trust for Scotland. Friendly assistance was given to me by L. L. Ardern, the late librarian of Broughton House, and currently by Frances Scott and Jim Allan. Also in Kirkcudbright I would like to thank Dr. David Devereux of the Stewartry Museum.

Smaller galleries have been most helpful. I wish to thank most sincerely Andrew McIntosh Patrick of The Fine Art Society, Richard Green, and Dr Robert Travers of Piano Nobile in London, and Ewan and Carol Mundy, William Hardie and Patrick Bourne in Scotland.

Private owners have always appreciated the paintings of Bessie MacNicol, and present-day owners have been most cooperative in allowing their pictures to be photographed. Most have preferred to remain anonymous; I am grateful to them all for their help. I would also like to thank R. Marilynn Muirhead for her fine photography.

Jude Burkhauser raised sponsorship for the important exhibition held in Glasgow in 1990 *'Glasgow Girls': Women in Art 1880-1920*. From surplus funds administered by Glasgow School of Art I was awarded £500 towards this book. I would like to thank Jude most sincerely for her championship of Glasgow women artists, and also Ray McKenzie, Department of Historical and Critical Studies at Glasgow School of Art, for my 'Glasgow Girls' research bursary.

ACKNOWLEDGEMENTS

Thanks are due to the following who have contributed assistance in many different ways: Hildegarde Berwick, Alison Brown, Bill Buchanan, Colin Donald, Ian McKenzie Smith, David Patterson, Mary-Jane Selwood, Joanna Soden and Winnie Tyrrell, with very special thanks to Una Rota for her interest over the years, and to Bill Smith for editing and designing this book and at a critical point for saving the day.

Finally I would like to thank members of the artist's family living on both sides of the Border, who have given me great encouragement, as well as my own family, who have been patient and supportive.

AILSA TANNER
Helensburgh, June 1998

INTRODUCTION

Some years ago I came into the possession of a bulky, oblong photograph album, which was quite blank apart from a few loose, assorted photographs inside. There was nothing remarkable about this empty album, but on the spine in gold letters were the words *PICTURES BY BESSIE MACNICOL*.

For some time I had been trying to obtain information on this artist, but was increasingly frustrated by lack of success. I had seen nine precious letters sent by her to Edward Atkinson Hornel, which are still in Broughton House, the fine eighteenth century house in the quiet High Street of Kirkcudbright where he lived from 1900. Hornel never threw anything away, for which we must be very grateful. These letters were all written in one year of her life, from December 1896 to December 1897. I had also seen an interesting book of photographs, which is still in family hands. Most of these were taken by her husband Alexander Frew, a good photographer. They had been shot in 1897, two years before their marriage, in his own house and garden in Helensburgh. Others were taken on holidays at Crail and Ardrishaig. Elsewhere is a single page from another letter by her to Hugh Hopkins, and that is all. I have not found any other letters by her or to her, no diaries, not a single sketchbook, and little trace of a lifetime's accumulation of odds and ends that help to fill out our knowledge and appreciation of a person's life and character.

I had hoped that the photographs lying in the empty album would add to my knowledge, but most were of canal scenes of the Low Countries, probably taken in Belgium or Holland, and I do not know if Bessie MacNicol had ever been there. There were a few others taken in Italy, the impressive ruins of the Temple at Paestum south of Naples, and some rural village scenes. They looked as if they had been taken by someone with an artist's eye who was also interested in photography. Could they too have been taken by her husband Alexander Frew and had she been to Italy as well?

These questions can never be answered as there is no one alive now with direct memories of this artist, but I have tried to fill that empty book with as much information as possible, and above all to illustrate it, as I think was intended, with reproductions of Bessie MacNicol's beautiful, vital paintings accomplished in her very short working life of little more than ten years. The critics were not kind to begin with, but notice was taken of her even for the wrong reasons. Her strong, vigorous oil-painting technique earned praise because it was masculine in style. Then she exhibited delicate watercolours, which were nothing if not feminine.

Today, we can accept that Bessie MacNicol was a most talented painter in her own right, who could express her personality in many differing forms. She was above all, as the Glasgow Art Club acknowledged in a last tribute to her at her funeral, ‘a true artist’.

1. FAMILY BACKGROUND

Elizabeth MacNicol was born on 15th July, 1869 at 352 St Vincent Street, Glasgow, the elder of twin daughters of Peter MacNicol, Headmaster of Anderston Burgh School, and his English wife Mary Ann Matthews, who had been married at Canton, Cardiff on 28th June, 1864. In 1865 twin boys were born, but one was stillborn and the survivor, Peter, died a year later. There was to be more tragedy in the family as Phoebe, the next child, died when she was five, and Mary, Bessie's own twin died from whooping cough when she was only six. It seems to have been a miracle that Bessie survived at all. We find it difficult to realise the high rate of infant mortality which existed in those days and which was to some extent accepted as inevitable. The pain of loss must have been great in the MacNicol family in 1876 when Mary died, as they had already lost twin sons and another daughter. However three girls did survive, Bessie who was now the eldest, Janet, or Jessie as she was called by her family, born on 9th May 1871 and the youngest, Minnie Phoebe, born on 9th September 1872. The latter was probably given Phoebe as a second name in memory of the sister who had died earlier the same year.

In 1871 the MacNicol family was living in the Anderston district of Glasgow at 186 North Street. This was in a tenement now demolished between Sauchiehall Street and Bath Street. According to the Census of that year the parents of Bessie's father were now staying with them in Glasgow, though the MacNicol family had been living in the Vale of Leven for two generations and before then at Drymen in the county of Stirling.

There were three generations bearing the name Peter MacNicol. The first was born in Drymen in 1777 and there are two entries of his birth in the Parish Records, one for Patrick and one for Peter. This was not uncommon at that time, when Gaelic forenames were given English equivalents. The shortened form of Padruig is Peadar, pronounced approximately Peter. This suggests that his parents were Gaelic speaking. His father John McNicol was a weaver, one of many in the village weaving goods for Glasgow. Later the population in the village dropped as many left to seek work in the mills of the Vale of Leven.

The Vale of Leven

During the 18th century the Vale of Leven, between Loch Lomond at Balloch and Dumbarton on the River Clyde, changed from a peaceful rural countryside to a polluted industrial area. The fast running, clear waters of the River Leven, haunt of salmon fishers, once flowed through green fields, where cloth was laid out on the grass to bleach by natural means. Channels leading from the river brought clean water to sprinkle over the cloth. In time chemicals superseded natural means for bleaching and, after the first print works were established in 1768, the water in the river became very polluted. It is interesting to find that the word 'field' was retained and the bleaching works and print works were called 'bleachfields' and 'printfields'. Calico printing and later silk dying developed during the century into a large industry. Population figures increased enormously as the workforce grew much larger.

The growth of population in the Vale associated with industrial growth led to many social problems. Tenements were hastily built to house the people, but there was no adequate provision for clean water and sanitation. That led to the spread of fever and even of cholera. The existing villages of Balloch and Bonhill were greatly enlarged, while new communities were formed at Alexandria, Jameston and Renton. The industrial growth reached its peak between 1860 and 1880, but after that there was a slow decline, hastened by both World Wars. The works at Alexandria survived until the 1960s, but since then the whole area has suffered recession and massive unemployment.

Patrick or Peter MacNicol made the move to the Vale of Leven towards the end of the 18th century and his marriage is recorded at Bonhill in 1800 to Elizabeth Tennant. Their eldest son Peter was born in the same year. This was Bessie MacNicol's grandfather, who became a master tailor at Bonhill, employing two men, and is later recorded as a teacher of English. He married Mary MacDougall from Cardross and their son Peter was born in 1839. This third generation Peter must have spent his childhood in the Vale of Leven, but he left it to live and work in Glasgow as a schoolteacher.

As Bessie MacNicol was later to show a real interest in clothes and costumes and in fashions, it is interesting to know that her grandfather was a tailor and her great great grandfather was a weaver. Similar craft backgrounds can be found in the families of other Glasgow artists, who very often had to take up other jobs and train in the early mornings and evenings until conditions became favourable for their full-time occupation as artists and artist designers.

2. GLASGOW 'THE SECOND CITY'

We don't know when Peter MacNicol, Bessie MacNicol's father, first left Bonhill for Glasgow, but it must have been before he was twenty, because in 1859 he was already Headmaster of Anderston Burgh School at 24 Catherine Street. He remained until 1882, when he was appointed Headmaster of Overnewton Public School, Lumsden Street. In the intervening years he married in 1864 Mary Ann Matthews at Canton, Cardiff. All six of their children were born in that period, but only three were still alive in 1882. Despite his demanding work of teaching and the stress of family tragedies in this period, he must have taken time to study for he graduated Master of Arts from the University of Glasgow in 1873. This degree must have been of great importance when applying for the post of Headmaster of Overnewton Public School.

Glasgow in the eighties was a busy, prosperous city with a growing sense of self confidence and pride in its position as 'Second City' of the Empire. With hindsight we can see there was too much reliance on heavy industries, shipbuilding, locomotive works and steel works. This led to the present day problems of deep recession and unemployment, but while there was growth there was optimism and success. At the same time Glasgow was not a very healthy city in which to bring up a young family. Housing was congested and the air very polluted, especially in foggy winter weather. Nevertheless it was an exciting time to be living there and the commercial prosperity found expression in huge exhibitions like the International Exhibition of 1888, which was itself a financial success. The profits helped to build the Art Galleries in Kelvingrove, which formed part of the larger and even more successful International Exhibition of 1901.

Great fortunes were made by successful industrialists and art and artists suddenly became necessary and important for the decoration of splendid new mansions. A group of painters whose work had been ridiculed earlier were being taken seriously by 1885. 'Glasgow Boys' was the name this loosely knit group of painters and one sculptor preferred to give themselves. They did not necessarily belong to Glasgow, but did exhibit in the spring exhibitions of the Glasgow Institute of the Fine Arts. They shared certain ideals in painting and above all a respect for painting in oils, but reacted against the historical costume pieces and sentimental genre scenes of their contemporaries. They shared admiration for the realist, village paintings of Jules Bastien-Lepage and for the works of James Abbott McNeill Whistler. They also shared the latter's love of 'things japanese.' One can imagine the excitement of young students as these innovative works were shown in the Institute. Francis Newbery, the Headmaster of

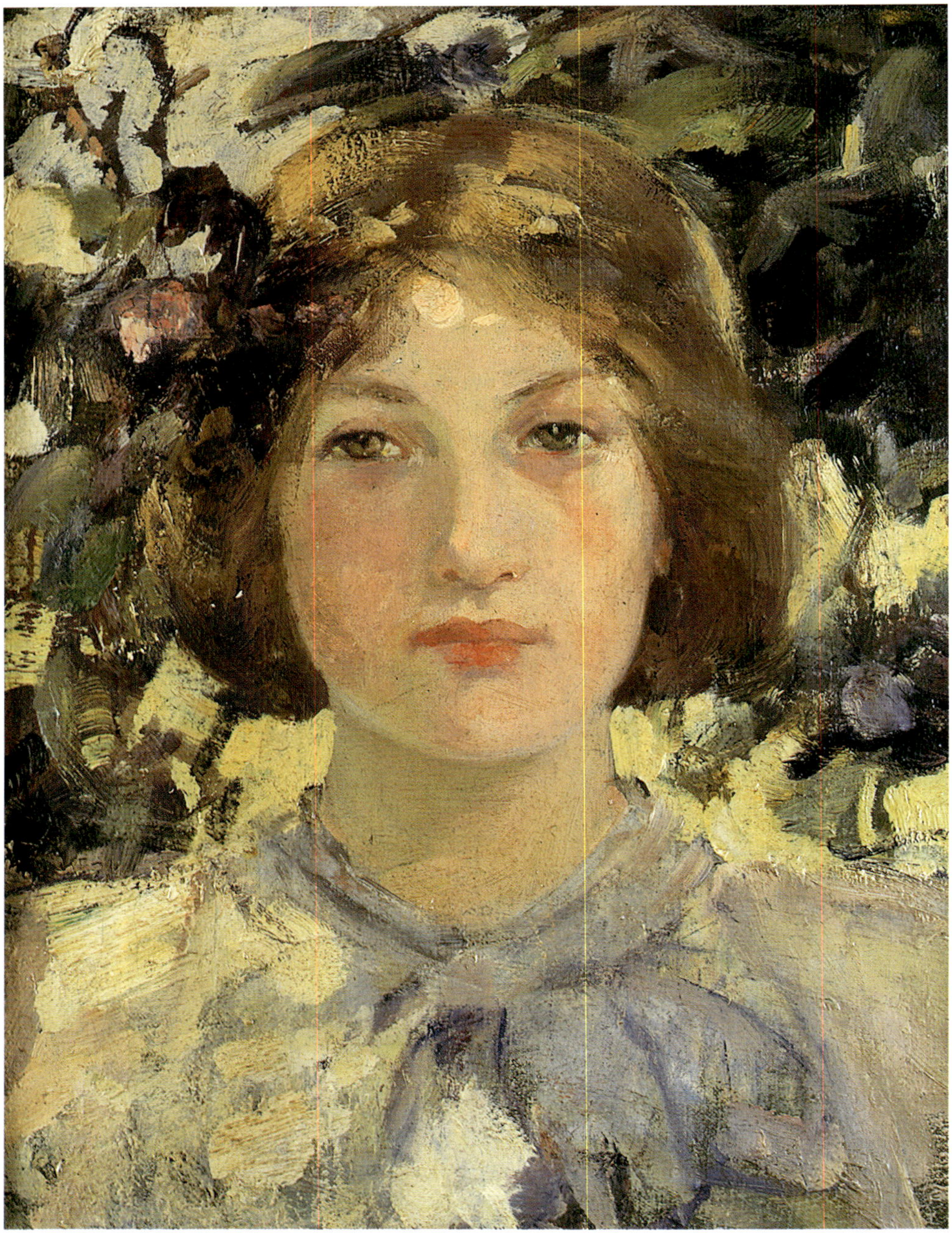

PLATE 1
Spring
Oil on canvas,
15¾x11¾
Private collection
(photo:R.M.Muirhead)

Glasgow School of Art, shared their admiration. He invited James Guthrie, later the accepted leader of the Boys, and his friends Edward Arthur Walton and John Lavery to become 'visitors' to the School in 1892.

Glasgow School of Art and Haldane Academy

Though the origins of Glasgow School of Art can be traced back to 1845 with the founding of a Government School of Design in order to improve the standard of design in manufactured goods, it was not until 1852 that it became a Government School of Art. In 1869 the School moved from

Ingram Street to a part of the Corporation Buildings in Rose Street, which at that time also housed the Art Collections of the City of Glasgow before they were moved to Kelvingrove. At present this building incorporates the McLellan Galleries.[1] It is to 1897, when the move was made to the first half of the building in Renfrew Street designed by Charles Rennie Mackintosh, that the present history of the Glasgow School of Art can be dated.

It was a good time to become a student of art even for a woman. Under Robert Greenlees and Thomas Simmonds, Headmasters of Glasgow School of Art at Rose Street before 1885, many women students had already been enrolled. At that time the MacNicol family was living at 14 Derby Terrace, near Kelvingrove Park, and it was with this address that Bessie MacNicol's name first appears in the Register of Glasgow School of Art in 1883. She was only fourteen years of age and apparently only stayed for one year, but nevertheless managed to gain a First Class Certificate in Freehand Drawing in that time. Her name does not appear again in the Register until 1887 when she was eighteen, so where did she go and what did she do in the intervening years?

St. George's School of Art

Glasgow School of Art and Haldane Academy was not the only teaching establishment for art in Glasgow at that time. In 1881 Robert Brydall, the second master at the School, had resigned at the same time as Robert Greenlees and had founded his own St. George's School of Art at 147 St. George's Road. A move was made in 1889 to 8 Newton Terrace, where the School continued until 1905, when Robert Brydall retired and moved to London.

In an article based on an interview with Mrs A. R. Laing, widow of the Glasgow painter James Garden Laing, Annie Rose Laing told the author James Shaw Simpson that St. George's School of Art was her first place of study.[2] She added that Bessie MacNicol was a fellow student, that the standard of instruction was not high, and that both she and Bessie MacNicol went on to become students at Glasgow School of Art. This is the only evidence we have that Bessie MacNicol studied at St. George's School of Art.

Queen Margaret College

Queen Margaret College, the first College for women in Scotland, was incorporated in 1883 from the Glasgow Association for the Higher Education of Women, which had been formed in 1877. Provision for instruction for women students in music and the visual arts was made in addition to academic subjects. The Annual Report for 1884 notes that James Campbell, Drawing Master to the High School of Glasgow, and his assistant Thomas Baird, architect, held classes on Monday, Wednesday and Friday evenings from 7 to 8.30 pm. But it was not until 1885 that Miss Janet Galloway, the devoted and untiring Secretary, wrote to Prof. Delamotte of King's College

London. It was due to his recommendation that G. Albert Laundy was appointed Lecturer in Art and Instructor in Drawing and Painting in the winter of 1885. Classes commenced in January 1886. Laundy was a pupil of Boulanger and Lefebre in Paris and his last appointment had been as Professor of Art at Bedford College, London. Not only did he instruct in Drawing and Painting, but, according to the advertisement, 'He will also accompany students to the Art Exhibitions, Annual and Permanent and give critical and explanatory instruction on the works exhibited.'[3]

Records of women students are held in the Archives of the University of Glasgow, but the name of Bessie MacNicol is not among them. The College itself was incorporated into the University of Glasgow in 1892 as its Department for Women. The first woman to obtain a medical degree from a Scottish University graduated in 1894.

The Glasgow Athenaeum

Percy Bate in his touching tribute to Bessie MacNicol after her untimely death in 1904 wrote:

> As a musician she was very gifted, as a painter richly equipped, and in either branch of art she would have succeeded, that painting was her final choice is our good fortune.[4]

While it may not be wise to accept this information from Percy Bate unreservedly, as he came to Glasgow only in 1900 to succeed Robert Walker as Acting Secretary of the Royal Glasgow Institute of Fine Art, it does prompt a consideration of music education in Glasgow around 1885-1887. An institution which catered for students in both music and art was the Glasgow Athenaeum at the top of Buchanan Street, later to become part of the Royal Scottish Academy of Music and Drama before the move to a new building in 1989. The Glasgow Athenaeum was founded in 1847 as an institution for adult education. Although the subjects covered were mathematics, languages and other disciplines associated with commerce, music and the fine arts were also taught. In 1885 there were classes in music for ladies, run by David B. Johnstone, a lecturer in the Church of Scotland Training College and organist of Lansdowne Church. These took place on Tuesday evenings from 7.30 till 9, the fee for 6 months being 5 shillings. Harmony & Musical Composition classes were held on Tuesdays and Thursdays between 6.30 and 7.30 and the fee for 6 months was higher at one guinea.[5]

The School of Music, with its first Principal Allan Macbeth, was not founded until 1891. Encouraged by its success, the School of Art was established a year later with Charles G. Kennaway as Principal and a staff of six teachers. The Prospectus gives the information that 'The Curriculum will cover the whole course of Art Instruction from Elementary Drawing to Painting from the Life, and there will be Classes for Modelling, Wood-

Carving, etc. The rooms have been specially fitted up for the purpose, and will be lighted by electricity on the newest method adopted in the Continental Art Schools.'[6]

Although these dates are too late for Bessie MacNicol to have studied at the School of Music, it is possible that she may have attended the earlier classes in music. Certainly her two younger sisters both became students at the School of Music. In 1892 Jessie MacNicol, with Allan Macbeth as tutor, obtained 1st Class Certificates in Pianoforte and Harmony and her younger sister Minnie a 2nd Class Certificate for solo singing. They both continued to study until 1894, Jessie MacNicol's name appearing in several programmes of students' concerts as soloist and accompanist. So there was certainly musical talent in the MacNicol family.

1 Hugh Ferguson, *Glasgow School of Art: The History*, Foulis Press of Glasgow School of Art 1995
2 James Shaw Simpson, *The Art of Mrs. A. R. Laing*, *Scottish Country Life* 1921 pp.260-1
3 University of Glasgow Archives
4 Percy Bate, *In Memoriam: Bessie MacNicol*, *Scottish Art and Letters*, vol.3 no.3 1904 p.198
5 Glasgow Athenaeum Prospectus 1885
6 Glasgow Athenaeum Prospectus 1892

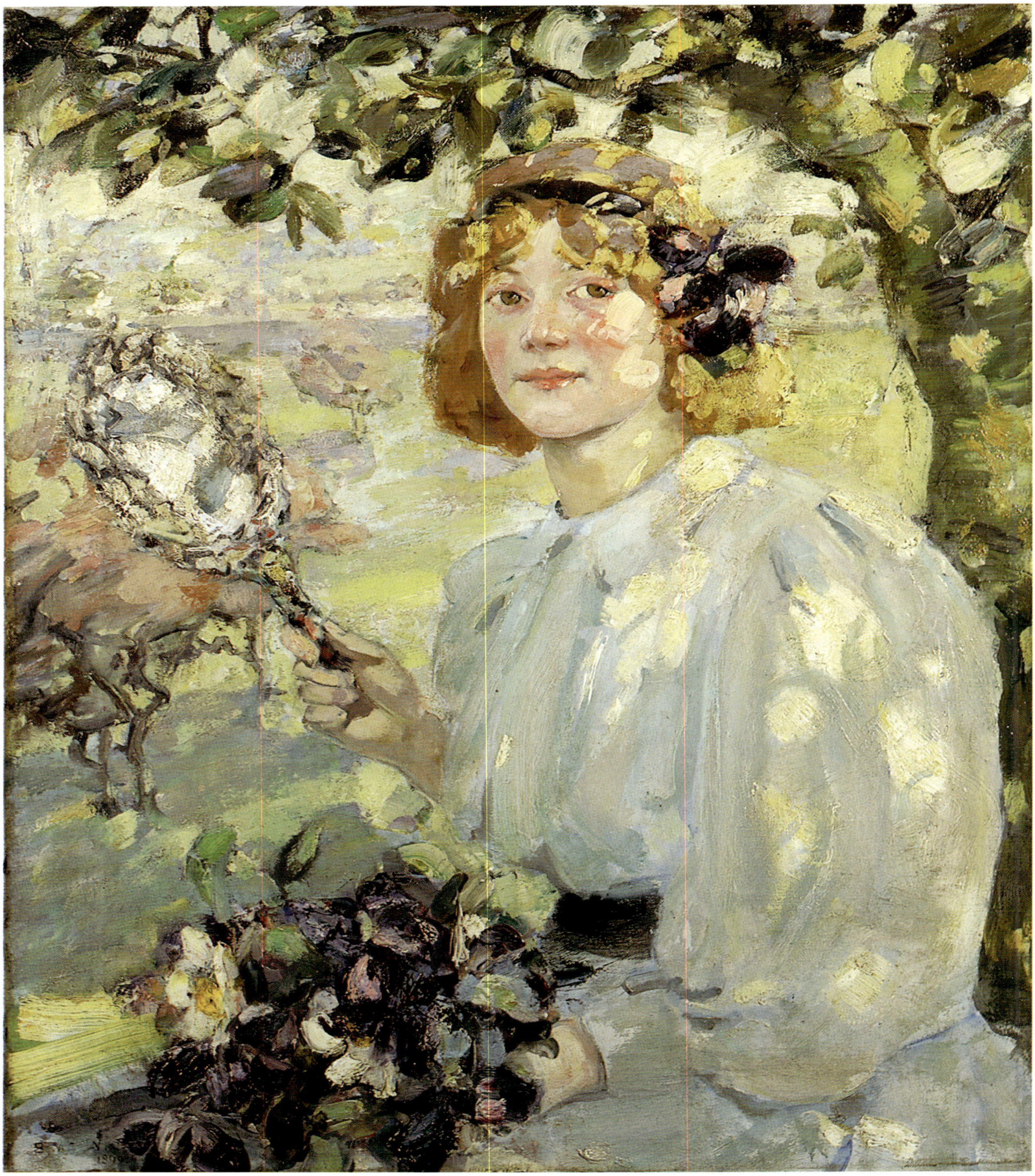

3. GLASGOW SCHOOL OF ART

Apart from the reminiscences of Annie Rose Laing already mentioned, there does not appear to be any other record of where Bessie MacNicol studied before she enrolled again at Glasgow School of Art and Haldane Academy in 1887 along with her younger sister Minnie. This time she stayed for the full course, though she does not appear to have qualified as a teacher of art. Her sister remained only for one year. At that time there are many instances of sisters enrolling together, perhaps as chaperones.

From 1887 until 1892 Bessie MacNicol studied under the benign and inspiring influence of the charismatic Headmaster Francis Henry Newbery, affectionately known to his students as 'Fra'. He had been appointed in 1885 and by 1887 had made his ideas and influence felt. He treated his women students in exactly the same way as the male students and until Maurice Greiffenhagen was appointed as Head of Painting in the School in 1905 'Fra' used to teach the painting students himself. He recognised the talent of this woman student, whose name appears in the Prize lists of 1889 and 1890. As well as a Bronze Medal for a Group in Oil Colours in 1890, Bessie was given a prize for Still Life, but this was cancelled as she had gained a National award. Annie Rose Low, who had been her fellow student at St George's School of Art and later married James Garden Laing, also had to forfeit her Still Life Prize. Surprisingly it was Low and not Bessie MacNicol who gained the coveted Haldane Travelling Bursary at the end of her studies in 1893. This was shared by Annie Rose Low and William Findlay and recorded in Glasgow School of Art Annual Report for 1893-94. Low was still in Paris when the Report was next published in 1895. The last record of Bessie MacNicol in the School of Art Register is for the session 1891-92. In that year the Haldane Bursary was won by Ella Alexander. The Award had been granted to a woman for the first time in 1889-90, when it was won by Stansmore Dean. Her painting career was somewhat restricted when she married the Glasgow Boy Robert Macaulay Stevenson and helped to bring up his young daughter Jean, who had been left motherless by the death of Stevenson's first wife.

There were several other notable students at the School of Art at the same time as Bessie MacNicol and Annie Rose Low. Among the men were Charles Rennie Mackintosh and David Gauld and among the women were Mrs Helen Law, whose second husband was Edward Arthur Walton, another Glasgow Boy. Among other contemporaries were the etcher Susan Crawford, Katharine Cameron, Frances and Margaret Macdonald and Jessie Keppie.

(opposite)
PLATE 2
Under the Apple Tree
Oil on canvas
29x25¼
Glasgow Museums: Art Gallery & Museum, Kelvingrove

THE GLASGOW KYRLE SOCIETY

In 1890 Fra Newbery became Convenor of the Decorative Branch of the Glasgow Kyrle Society.[1] The aim of this Society was 'to bring the influences of natural and artistic beauty home to the people.' The Decorative Branch arranged for the decoration of Mission Halls attached to churches and prisons, Institutions for the Deaf and Dumb, and Working Girls' Clubs. In the West of Scotland this work was not confined to Glasgow and some 'bright pictures' were sent to the little hospital at Portree on the Isle of Skye. The Kyrle Society also operated branches in London, Leicester and Birmingham. Similar work was carried out in Edinburgh by the Edinburgh Social Union. Phoebe Anna Traquair had painted the walls of the Mortuary Chapel of the Sick Children's Hospital in Edinburgh, the Song School of St Mary's Cathedral and was still engaged in the mammoth undertaking of painting the murals in the Catholic Apostolic Church in Mansfield Place.

When Fra Newbery was appointed Convenor, the list of Committee Members included several members of the Glasgow Society of Lady Artists, including the President Mrs Agnew, Mrs P. H. Aikman, a founder member, Mrs Paterson Wingate and Newbery's own wife Jessie. Architects John Honeyman and William Leiper were on the Committee too, together with the well known Glasgow artist David Murray before his move south to London.

Fra Newbery took his responsibilities very seriously. In 1890 he had arranged for five panels to be placed on the walls of the Prisoners' Aid Society's Hall in Duke Street. These were painted by the recently acknowledged Glasgow Boys, Walton, Henry, Roche, Corsan Morton and Nairn.[2] In 1889 the Merkland Street Mission Hall in Partick was decorated with three panels, the subjects taken from pictures by Jean Francois Millet including *The Angelus*. In this case the artists were three students of Glasgow School of Art, Annie Rose Low, Bessie MacNicol and Patrick William Orr. The 1890-91 Report notes 'They executed their work gratuitously, and to them the Committee gives its warmest thanks for the services thus rendered.'[3] Unfortunately nothing remains of these two buildings or presumably their contents.

LUNDIN LINKS

Fra Newbery's influence on his students was not confined to term time. Starting shortly after his appointment to Glasgow School of Art, he went to Lundin Links in Fife in the summer vacations. Fife, or Fifeshire as it was called then, was a favourite painting ground for artists. The quality of light was quite different from that of the West of Scotland, the weather was drier and, even more attractive, living there was cheaper. Lundin Links was where the artists stayed, but subjects were found all round the East Neuk. At that time the harbours were busy with fishing boats, and the fishermen's houses were attractive with red pantiled roofs. Much has been written about Cockburnspath and Kirkcudbright, but less is known about Lundin Links and its visiting artists.

The painters who gathered there were from both Glasgow and Edinburgh. Describing the Lundie Mill of 1892 James Mavor wrote:

> . . . Lundin Mills [sic] was a favourite spot for painters. Cameron lived there, and at that time Newbery and others used to spend the summer in the village.[4]

Neil Munro in *The Brave Days* was more specific:

> [Muirhead Bone] and his future brother-in-law Frank Dodd went to paint the red tile roofs of Largo and Kilrenny in Fifeshire because living was cheap there 12s a week for the pair of them! Forby in Fife they were in the stimulating company of Archie Kay and Fra Newbery, their old Art School teachers, Macaulay Stevenson, Coventry and many other Glasgow artists.[5]

It would seem that a very informal form of Summer School took place at Lundin Links, more a gathering of fellow artists, students and friends. This was centred on Craig Cottage, where Fra Newbery stayed after his marriage to Jessie Rowat in 1889. Women students could also join the group, chaperoned by one of the two women staff members, Miss Jessie R. Allan and Miss Isabella Anderson. It is very likely that Bessie MacNicol stayed at Lundin Links at that time and returned for more than one summer.

It was there that Bessie MacNicol made studies for the painting *The Goose Girl* dated 1898 (pl.39), which was first exhibited the following year at the Glasgow Institute and then at the Women's International Exhibition at Earl's Court in 1900. Miss Jean Stewart Brown, daughter of Mary, the little girl who was used as the model for *The Goose Girl*, has told the author that it must have been in 1890 or 1891, when her mother and aunt were staying with their grandmother at Lundin Links while their own mother was working in Edinburgh. Mary's older sister Jean was asked to pose, but could not keep still. So instead Mary stood in what was known as 'The Fir Wood', opposite the Lundin Links Hotel, and was rewarded by a present of ribbons from Bessie MacNicol brought the next summer. Mary remembered the beautiful crisp blouses that Bessie MacNicol wore and the man's cap with her hair pushed inside, as well as Fra Newbery walking arm in arm with Jessie on the beach at Lower Largo.

Paris

After 1892, probably with the encouragement of Fra Newbery, Bessie MacNicol went to Paris to attend classes at the Académie Colarossi in the Rue de la Chaumière on the Left Bank. She was then twenty-three years of age. The only account of her stay is given by Percy Bate, writing in 1904 after her death:

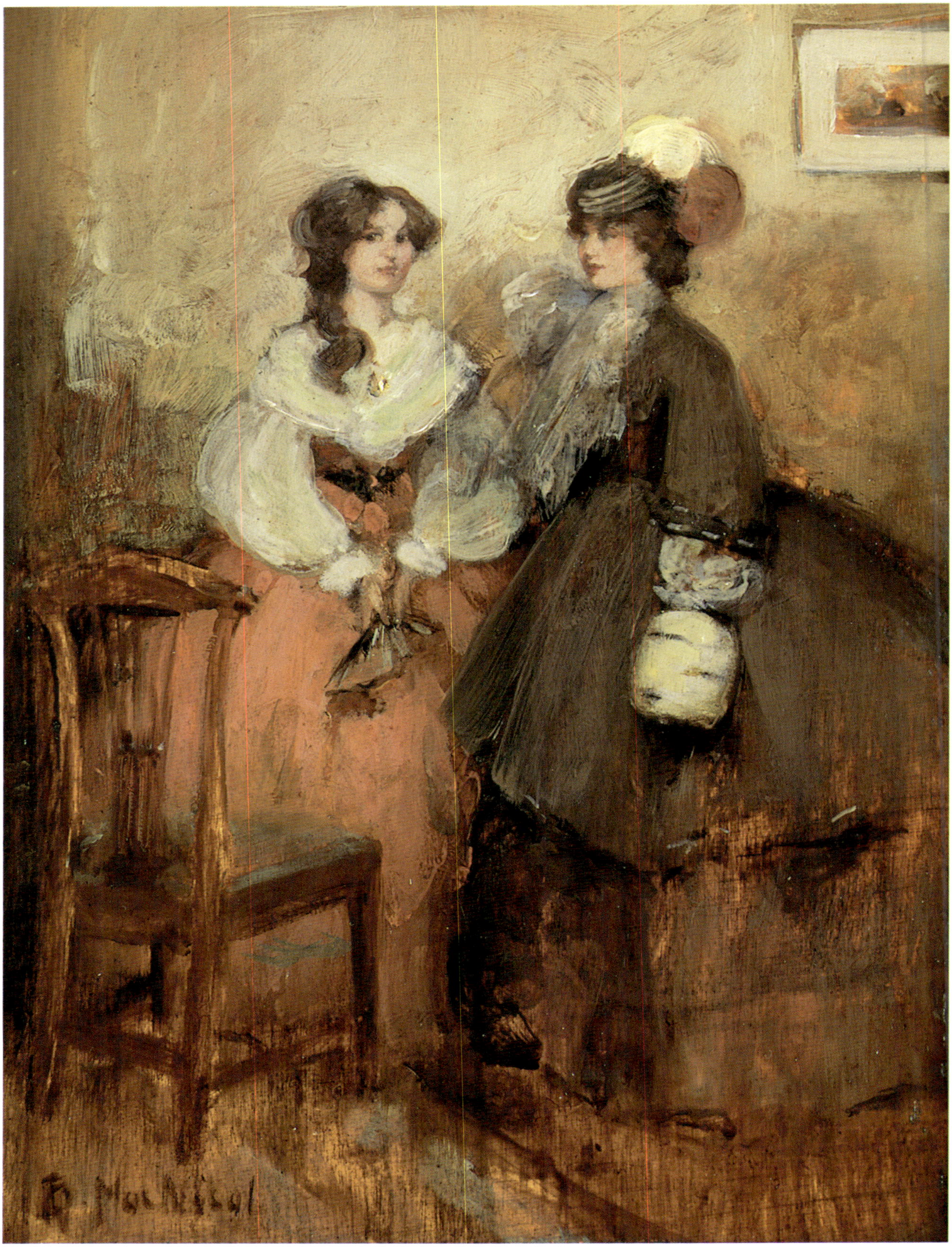

(opposite)
PLATE 3
Gossips
Oil on panel
12x10
Lord and Lady Macfarlane of Bearsden
(photo: R.M.Muirhead)

> . . . she only stayed a short time, and did but little work, for she found that her individuality was not given a chance; she was restrained and repressed rather than encouraged, and her study there resolved itself more into a mental training rather than a manual one. She haunted the galleries, moved by the masterpieces of Vandyke, Velasquez and Botticelli.'[6]

The tutors at the Académie Colarossi included August Courtois and René Prinet.

It is tantalising that there is no further information on Bessie MacNicol's stay in Paris. We would like to know if she went to exhibitions and what she thought of contemporary work in Paris. Was she in Paris at the same time as fellow student Annie Rose Low or was she there on her own? Low gave her tutors as Jean Paul Laurens and Aman-Jean, but like Bessie MacNicol she did not feel that she had gained from study in Paris.[7]

There were other Scottish artists studying and working in Paris at that time. Robert Brough, William James Yule, John Duncan Fergusson and Samuel John Peploe were in Paris for periods from 1891 to 1894. Peploe is on record as working at the Académie Colarossi.[8]

1 Glasgow Kyrle Society, Annual Report 1890
2 *Quiz* 5 July 1889
3 Glasgow Kyrle Society, Annual Report 1890/91
4 James Mavor, *My Window on the Street of the World* 1923 p.235
5 Neil Munro, *The Brave Days* 1931
6 Percy Bate, op. cit. p.198
7 James Shaw Simpson, op. cit. p.260
8 Roger Billcliffe, *The Scottish Colourists* 1989 p.15

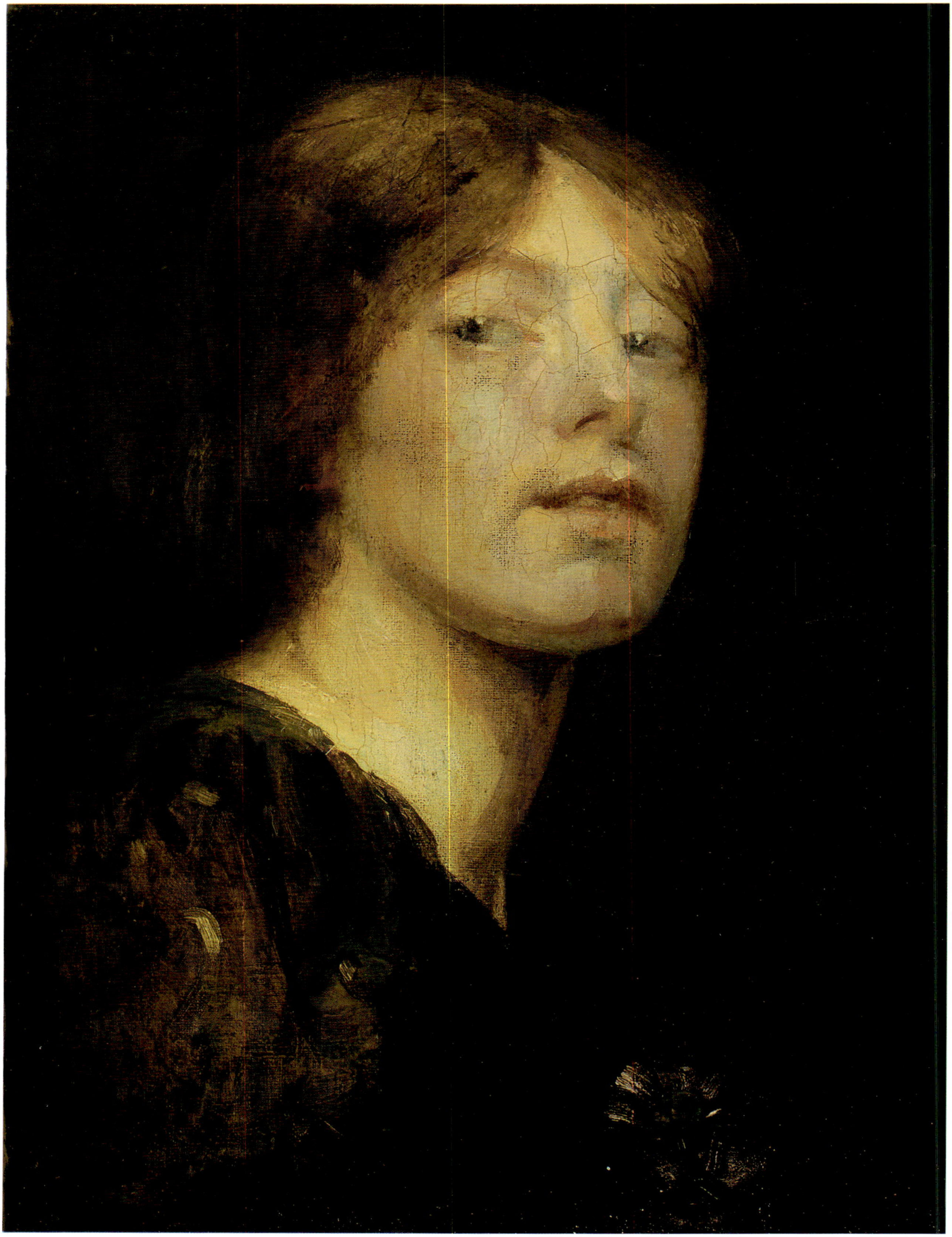

4. EARLY WORKS

A French Girl

Either in Paris or on her return Bessie MacNicol painted two works which obviously have a connection with her stay in France. *A French Girl* (pl.8) was exhibited at the Glasgow Institute in 1895 and was probably painted in the summer of the previous year. A single page of a letter survives, written by Bessie at Crail to Hugh Hopkins, whom she addresses as 'Dear Hugo'. She wrote 'I have done a head of a French Tottie however, which is rather jolly, pretty I mean!'[1] There is a little pen sketch of a girl's head on the page (pl.7), which relates unmistakably to *A French Girl,* and an added note states 'Heliotrope sleeves – needless to say!' This must refer to some shared joke – a favourite colour or a favourite dress.

In 1904 Percy Bate wrote:

> At the hands of a sympathetic hanger [the hangers of the 1895 Institute exhibition were George Henry, Robert McGown Coventry and John Wordie] it was placed as it deserved and art lovers at once saw that in Bessie MacNicol a new artistic force had arisen in Glasgow.[2]

There is little evidence in the press reviews of the exhibition to support this

(opposite)
PLATE 4
Self-Portrait
Oil on canvas
16x12
Glasgow Museums:
Art Gallery &
Museum, Kelvingrove
(photo: Sotheby's)

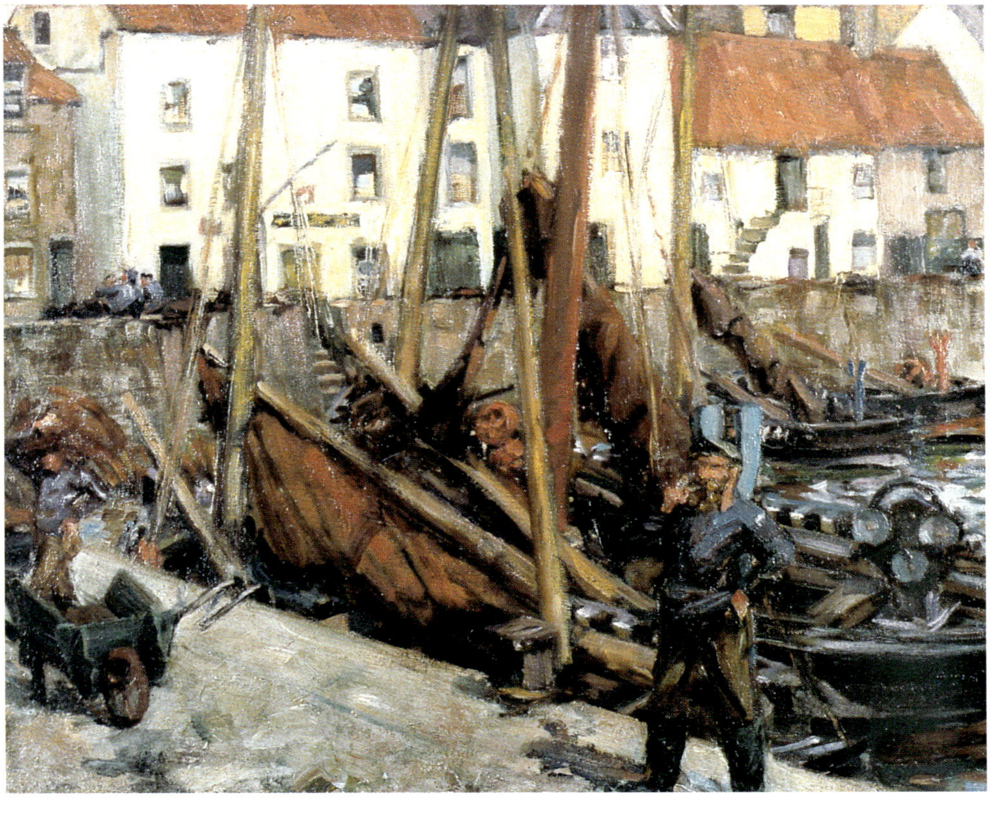

PLATE 5
St Monance
Oil on canvas
16x19¾
Private collection
(photo: Piano Nobile
Fine Paintings)

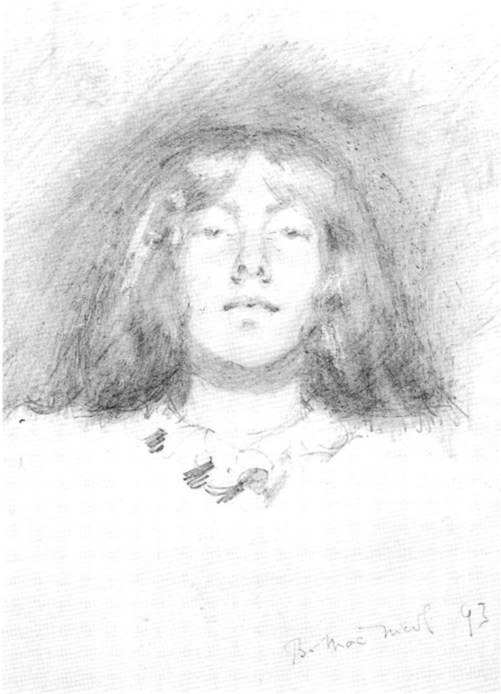

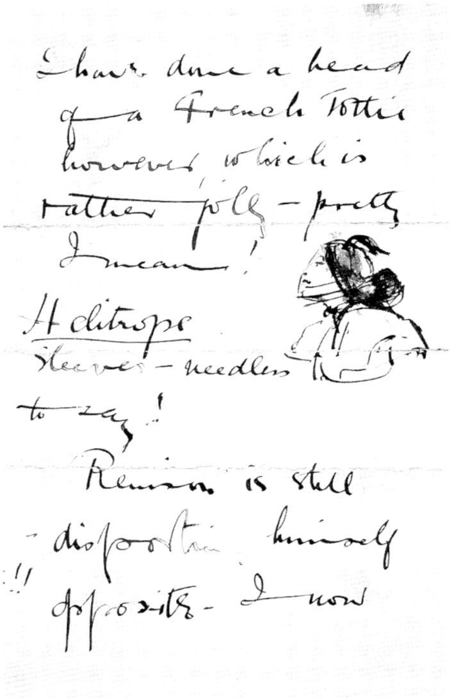
I have done a head
of a French Tottie
however, which is
rather jolly – pretty
I mean!
Heliotrope
sleeves – needless
to say!
Renison is still
disporting himself
opposite – I now

(left)
PLATE 6
Self-Portrait
Pencil
Private collection
(photo: A.Gorzkoski)

(right)
PLATE 7
Sketch in letter
Pen & ink
Private collection
(photo: R.M.Muirhead)

claim, which must have been gathered from the memories of friends. However before the exhibition opened *The Bailie* did note that '. . . Miss Bessie MacNicol has sent in the study of a head, decorative in style . . .'[3] and the review of the exhibition in the *North British Daily Mail* stated: '. . . Miss B.MacNicol's head (47) is chic and clever, though the almost horizontal extension of the neck is a little startling.'[4]

For an early work *A French Girl* is an astonishing display of virtuosity. It shows self-confidence in its assured brushwork and great originality in its composition. 'Portrait' is a term traditionally used to describe an upright rectangle, as compared to 'landscape', but *A French Girl* has been painted on a canvas whose breadth is greater than its height.

The rather exaggerated shape of the neck is most intriguing. As a painter Bessie MacNicol was naturally interested in the work of other artists. She may have looked closely at the work of Ingres in the Louvre and, nearer home, at that of her contemporary, Edward Atkinson Hornel. In some of Hornel's paintings dating from before his visit to Japan with George Henry in 1893-94, and used many times later, is the motif of a girl's head in profile leaning backwards. It can be seen in *The Brook* of 1890 (pl.9), exhibited at the Glasgow Institute in 1891, which was bought by Herbert J. MacNair, and also in *The Silk Shop*, a Japanese extravaganza painted in 1896. Bessie MacNicol used it again in a work painted in Kirkcudbright probably in 1896 (though the painting is dated 1897) of young girls dancing round with white blossoms. One of the girls with dark hair has her head tilted back in this position. This is

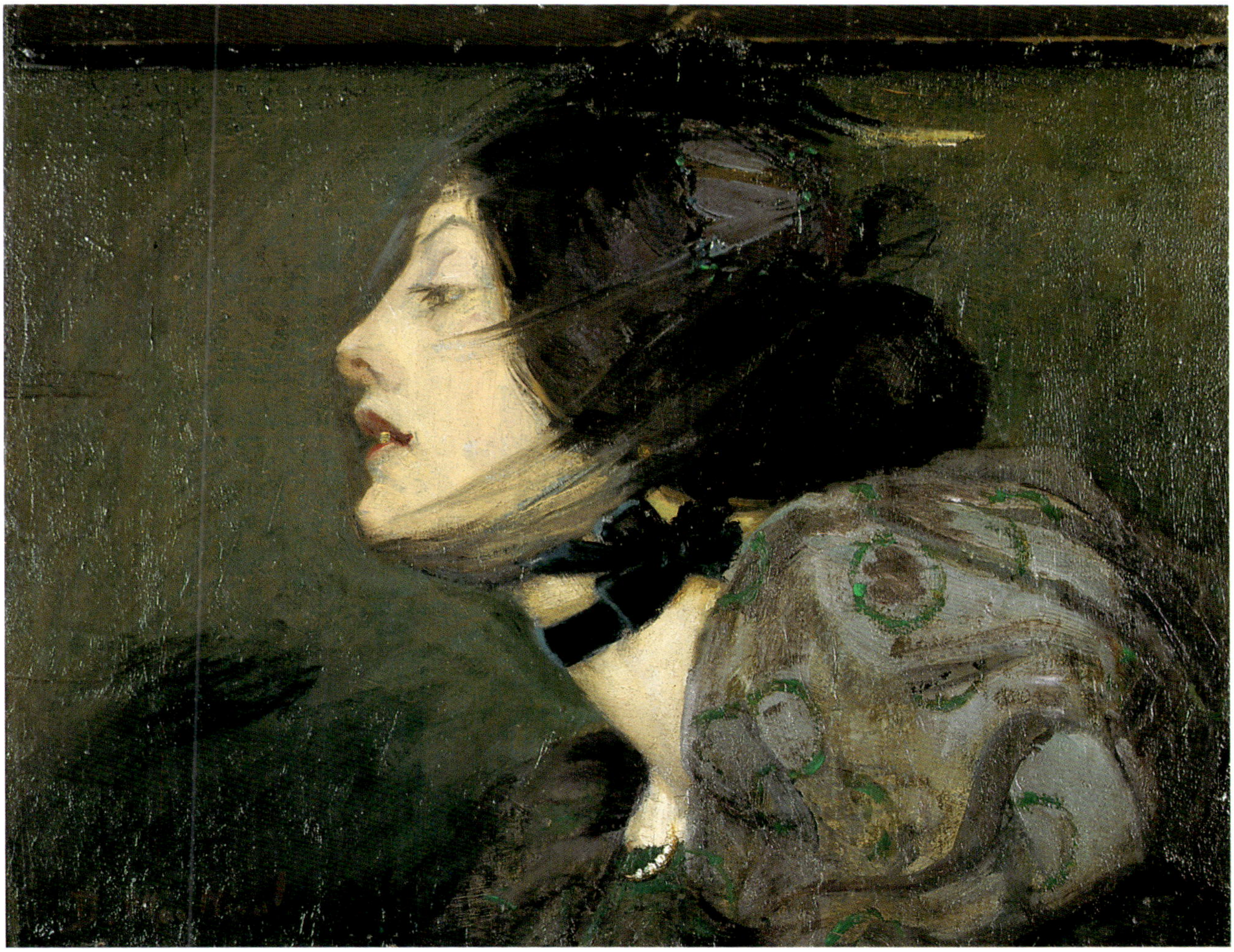

PLATE 8
A French Girl
Oil on canvas
15x19
Private collection
(photo: Sotheby's)

arguably the painting sent by her to Venice in 1899 and called *A Battle of Flowers*, no.31 in the 3rd Biennale catalogue.

A French Girl was bought from the Institute Exhibition by Miss Robin, Broompark, Largs, but later it came into the possession of Hugh Hopkins, who succeeded his father of the same name in his antiquarian book shop in Exchange Square. The inner room of the shop was a favourite meeting place for book lovers in Glasgow, where discussions took place accompanied by a glass of sherry. Hugh Hopkins was related to the Keppie family; the architect John Keppie and his sister Jessie were his first cousins. Bessie MacNicol may have been referring to Hopkins in a letter written to Hornel in 1897: '. . . I have been having some stormy scenes with an old beau this week.'[5]

Self-Portrait

In her self-portrait (pl.4), which may have been the *Study of a Head* exhibited as not for sale at the Glasgow Institute of 1893, her own head is tilted slightly

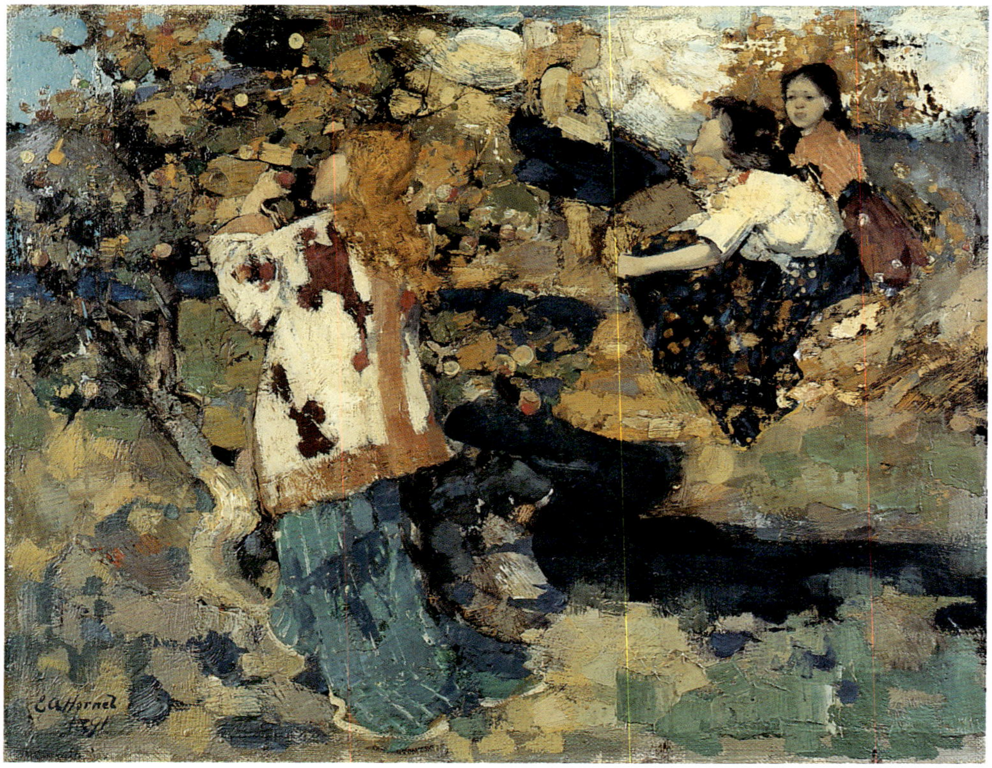

PLATE 9
E. A. Hornel
The Brook
Oil on canvas
16x19¾
Hunterian Art Gallery, University of Glasgow

back. She appears to view herself – and the onlooker – with a quizzical, almost supercilious expression. What a splendid portrait this is, most beautifully painted in low tones and restrained colour. It has the appearance of an old master and was probably painted shortly after her return from Paris. Percy Bate has mentioned that she was interested in Vandyke, but the lighting and the dark background suggest an interest in the work of Rembrandt. John Keppie, who owned this painting, lent it to the 1910 Secession Exhibition in Vienna. When he died in 1945, he left it to Glasgow Art Gallery along with another work by Bessie MacNicol *A Girl of the 'Sixties'*. The only pencil drawing that has surfaced so far is also of herself. It is dated 1893, but looks as if it was drawn at an earlier date (pl.6). *Portrait* exhibited at the Institute in 1896 was another self-portrait and was noticed in the Glasgow weekly periodical *Quiz*:

> . . . not without merit. Her own eyes are beautiful, and she has drawn them well, but why should she like Walt Whitman 'celebrate' herself, the example of Rembrandt notwithstanding – and give us portrait after portrait of herself.[6]

Study of a Head was the only painting shown by her in Glasgow in 1893, and in the same year she exhibited at the Royal Academy in London for the first and last time. In the catalogue the painting is titled *Fifeshire Interior*, but Percy Bate in writing of the picture calls it a low toned study of *A Carpenter's Shop*.[7] This is interesting for Fra Newbery had exhibited a painting with the

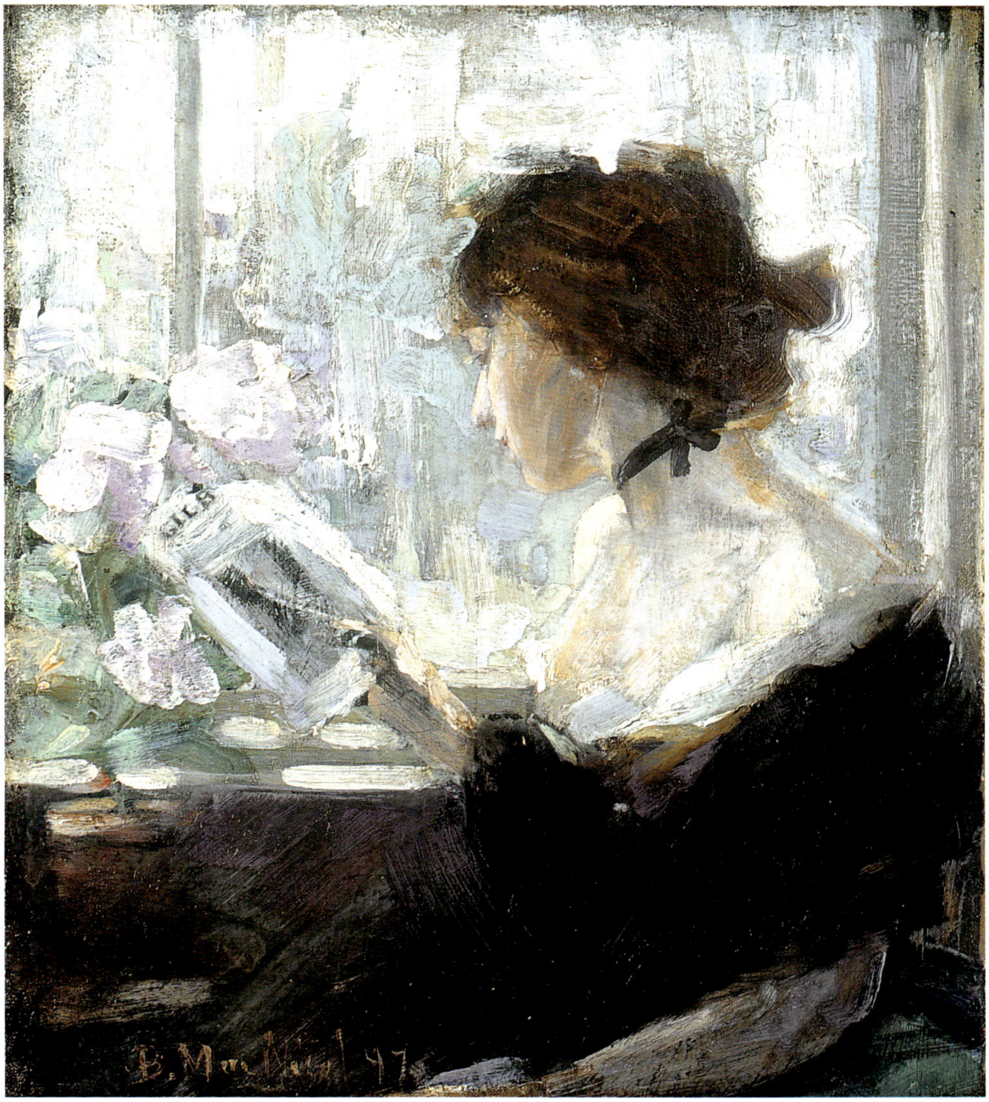

PLATE 10
Elizabeth
Oil on canvas
14x12
Private collection
(photo: Ewan Mundy Fine Art)

same title at the Glasgow Institute in 1892. It seems very likely that both pictures were of the same Fifeshire subject, painted about 1891 while they were at Lundin Links.

In 1894 she exhibited *St Monance* (pl.5), a quayside scene which is probably the painting of the same subject discovered under *A French Girl* when it was cleaned in 1981. Certainly, if the painting was not sold in 1894, it was natural for Bessie MacNicol to use the frame again the following year. That might account for the unconventional shape of the portrait, which could have been made to fit the frame. There are several other paintings of Fife harbours recorded, but not so far traced, which must have been painted at the same time.

The charming small painting *Elizabeth* (pl.10) is dated 1897, but one feels it is related to her stay in Paris. It shows a young girl reading by a window, and the black choker is almost identical to that in *A French Girl.* One can only assume that the paper, on which one can see the letters 'Gil B', must be the Parisian periodical *Gil Blas.* However the style of painting has changed. Lighter colours are used and that must have been as a result of what happened in 1896, the year she went to Kirkcudbright and came under the influence of the work of E. A. Hornel.

1 Private Collection
2 Percy Bate, op. cit. p.198
3 *The Bailie* 16 January 1895 p.10
4 *North British Daily Mail* 23 April 1895 p.2
5 Bessie MacNicol letter no.2, Broughton House, Kirkcudbright
6 *Quiz* 19 March 1896 p.16
7 Percy Bate, op.cit. p.199

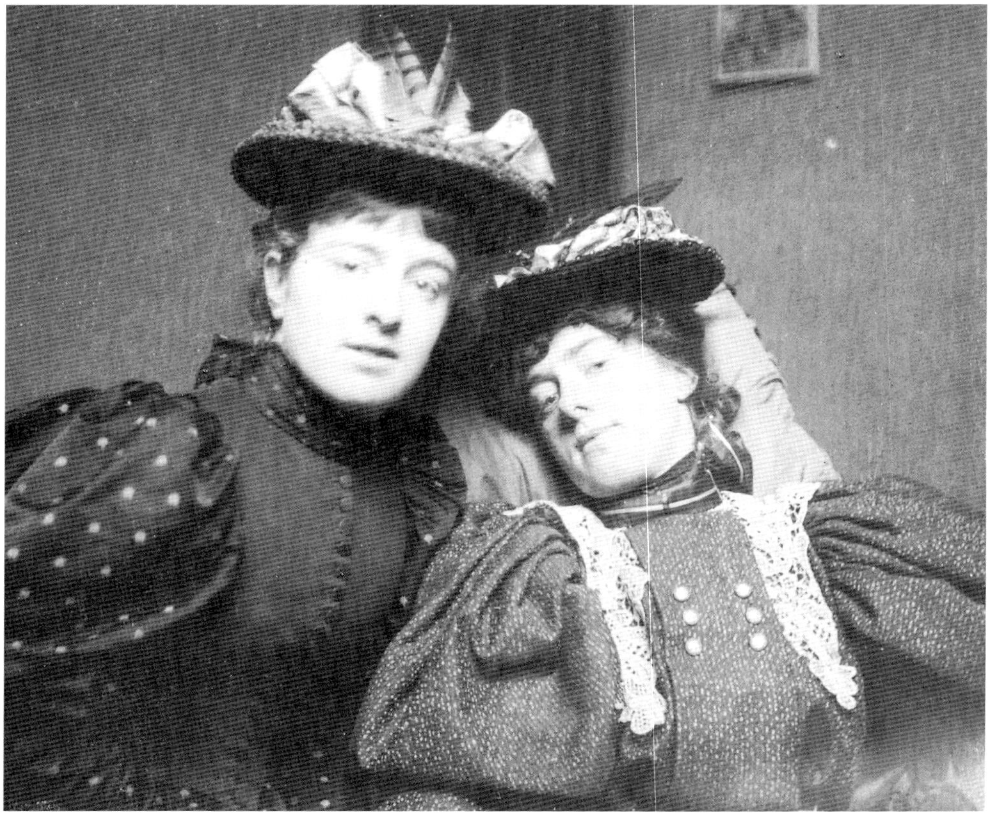

PLATE 11
Jessie and Bessie MacNicol

5. KIRKCUDBRIGHT 1896

It is not known when Bessie MacNicol first went to Kirkcudbright. We do know she was there in 1896, when she painted a portrait of Hornel, and that she returned for further visits in the following year and possibly later. Her name appears in the Visitors' Book of the Stewartry Museum on 16th September 1896, and in the Day Book of The Scottish Gallery in Edinburgh, at that time owned by McOmish Dott, in which her address is given as 'Kirkcudbright'. Thanks to her friendship with Edward Atkinson Hornel and the nine letters written by her to him from Christmas 1896 to Christmas 1897, we know more about this year than any others of her life.

At that time Kirkcudbright was a favourite town for artists, especially those from Glasgow, as it was reasonably accessible by train via Dumfries. This little town by the mouth of the Dee, set in the attractive Galloway landscape, pastoral yet rugged, was a welcome change from dirty, smoky Glasgow. Hornel was the leader of the 'Kirkcudbright School' as W. E. Henley called it. Other resident artists were his brother-in-law William Mouncey, Thomas Bromley Blacklock and William MacGeorge. Among the migrant summer visitors at various times were Alexander Roche, James Whitelaw Hamilton, David Gauld, John Reid Murray, Thomas Corsan Morton and Harry Spence, the latter called 'the Josser' by his friends for some reason now lost to us. James Guthrie and George Henry were in Kirkcudbright in 1886 and perhaps the previous year. In 1889 Henry painted his important and seminal picture *A Galloway Landscape*. He was then closely associated with Hornel, whose home was at the 'Kirk' as the town was affectionately called by the painters.[1]

Hornel and Henry collaborated on two large paintings, *The Druids – Bringing in the Mistletoe* in 1890 and *The Star in the East* in 1891. The former is a rich decorative fantasy in oils with gold embellishments, portraying a legendary ceremony of Galloway's remote past. In the many letters written by Henry to Hornel, which are now in the care of The National Trust for Scotland at Broughton House in Kirkcudbright, there is evidence that while Henry was in Glasgow he was dependent on Hornel to supply him with sketches of trees and berries, and on one occasion he even asked for 'a winding burn'. Just such a winding burn plays an important part in *A Galloway Landscape* and is very oriental in style. Hornel was interested in Japanese art long before he and Henry visited the Far East. They did in fact make the journey together in 1893, sponsored by the art dealer Alexander Reid and others, including William Burrell. They stayed in Japan for nine months, though not always together. After their return to Scotland in July 1894 Hornel held a most successful exhibition in Glasgow at Alexander

Reid's *La Société des Beaux Arts* the following year, when almost all his work was sold. Their friendship cooled after 1895, but not with dramatic suddenness. The last dated letter from Henry to Hornel now at Broughton House was written on 12th August 1896, but it is doubtful if Henry painted in Kirkcudbright after that date.

Both painters suffered as a result of this rift in their friendship. Hornel had keen intelligence and many interests. He was fascinated by the Orient and also in the distant past of Galloway. Henry was the more instinctive painter and, while they exchanged ideas and influenced each other, they both gained in choice of subjects and in painterly quality. Henry joined Guthrie and Walton in London towards the end of the century, where he became successful as a society painter and as an exhibitor at the Royal Academy. Hornel stayed in Scotland at Kirkcudbright, continuing to paint the same subjects for the rest of his life, but without the initial inspiration.

A Galloway Landscape

Like Henry, Bessie MacNicol also painted a scene entitled *A Galloway Landscape* (pl.12). According to Glasgow Art Gallery's *Summary Catalogue of British Oil Paintings*, this work is dated 1889, which scarcely seems possible as she was still a student then, but the ambiguous figures could read 1897. The painting is weak in design, compared with the more assured decorative vision of Henry, but it has its own charm. The landscape is a more open one across a valley and, given a high horizon, the eye is made to look downwards. There

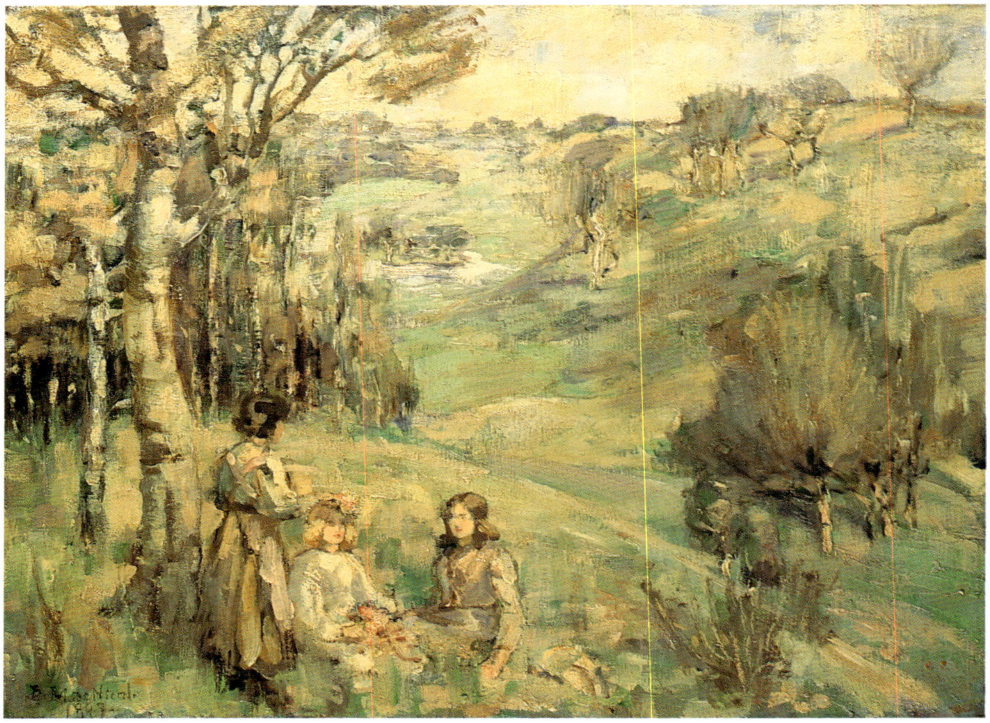

PLATE 12
A Galloway Landscape
Oil on canvas
20x27
Glasgow Museums: Art Gallery & Museum, Kelvingrove

PLATE 13
JAMES GUTHRIE
Midsummer
Oil on canvas
39x49
Royal Scottish Academy
Diploma Collection
(photo: Tom Scott)

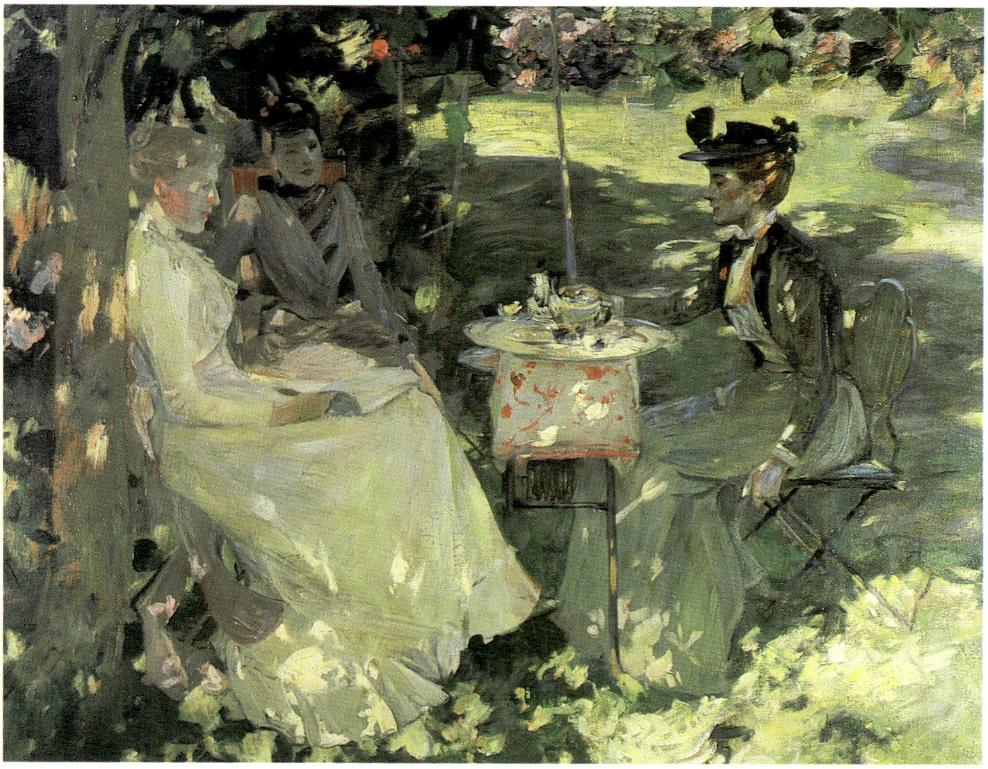

have been many theories about the location of Henry's painting, which with the everchanging effect of growth over the years is now impossible to identify with certainty, if in fact it ever existed in reality. The same can be said of MacNicol's painting. Is it the valley of the Dee, or Bombie Glen near Kirkcudbright? The trees are birches and relatively small, their stunted growth suggesting higher ground open to winds from the sea. Galloway is full of contrasts. There are tall forest trees and lush growth in sheltered places helped by the milder climate in winter, but also outcrops of rock, poorer pasture and scrubby growth in less favoured places.

The weakness of the composition lies mainly in the somewhat unresolved painting of the three figures in the foreground, which, although they do give a sense of scale, have been placed too near the foot of the picture. By this time the Glasgow Boys had developed an interest in painting *en plein air*, a favourite subject being figures in a landscape. Following the lead of Jules Bastien-Lepage, James Guthrie had painted the farmworkers of East Lothian and other ordinary people at work in the fields. Even his children are depicted picking apples in an orchard or cutting greens in a kitchen garden. Bessie MacNicol herself had already made studies of this type and was later to exhibit a painting in this genre entitled *The Goose Girl*. However, like several other painters working in the south west, her figures in *A Galloway Landscape* are included to add to the idyllic character of the landscape and to suggest leisure and enjoyment rather than work. Alexander

Roche painted *Spring Time*, which was exhibited at the Glasgow Institute in 1895, a somewhat similar subject to Bessie MacNicol's *A Galloway Landscape*.[2] It was a subject which was also tackled by William MacGeorge and William Mouncey, both residents of Galloway, whose work she knew well. Later Hornel himself confined his subject matter almost exclusively to small girls playing in woodlands, by the lakeside or by the seashore at Brighouse Bay. There is evidence to suggest that around 1896 some of the models used by him were tinker children, who lived with their families in an encampment on the Doon, a sandy beach on the north shore of the Dee estuary. Bessie MacNicol may also have used these children as models for a time. Later Hornel was to depend on photographs of local Kirkcudbright girls for his subjects.

(opposite)
PLATE 14
Apple Blossom
Oil on canvas
24x20
Private collection
(photo: R.M.Muirhead)

Under the Apple Tree

The figure crowned with flowers in the centre of Bessie MacNicol's *A Galloway Landscape* is an interesting reminder of the young girl in *Under the Apple Tree* (pl.2), now in Glasgow Art Gallery. This important painting must have been started in 1896 for this date is inscribed on it. However, as was quite customary with her, the painting was probably altered later as it also bears the date '1899'. It is one of a large group of paintings of a single figure of a girl under a tree with sun shining through the leaves, dappling her face and dress. In this case there is a distant landscape behind. A painting which is still in the possession of the artist's family may be the first of this group (pl.14), probably a portrait of a family member or a close friend. In this study the trunk of the tree is not seen, only a leafy bough, and the horizon is placed lower on the canvas. Patches of sunlight can be seen, however, on the girl's neck and dress. This painting may be the work titled *Apple Blossom* or is perhaps a study for that painting.

The effect of sunlight through trees had been explored by James Guthrie in *Midsummer* (pl.13), which was painted in 1892. Three girls are having tea in a garden. On the left is Maggie Hamilton, the elder sister of James Whitelaw Hamilton, a fellow painter with the Glasgow Boys at Cockburnspath. In the centre is her sister Mary Jane, and Hannah Walton, sister of another Glasgow Boy Edward Arthur Walton, is pouring out tea on the right. The garden is that of Thornton Lodge, the Hamiltons' house in Helensburgh. The day is warm and they are seated in the shade. The sun filters through the leaves and is seen in flecks in the shadow on the lawn and on the dresses of the girls, leading the viewer's eye round the painting.

George Moore was charmed by this painting. His description of it has for us the same nostalgic period flavour of the painting itself:

> . . . A garden in the summer's very moment of complete efflorescence, a bower of limpid green, here and there interwoven with red flowers. And three ladies are there with their tiny Japanese tea table. One dress – that on the left – is white, like a lily, drenched with green shadows, the dress on

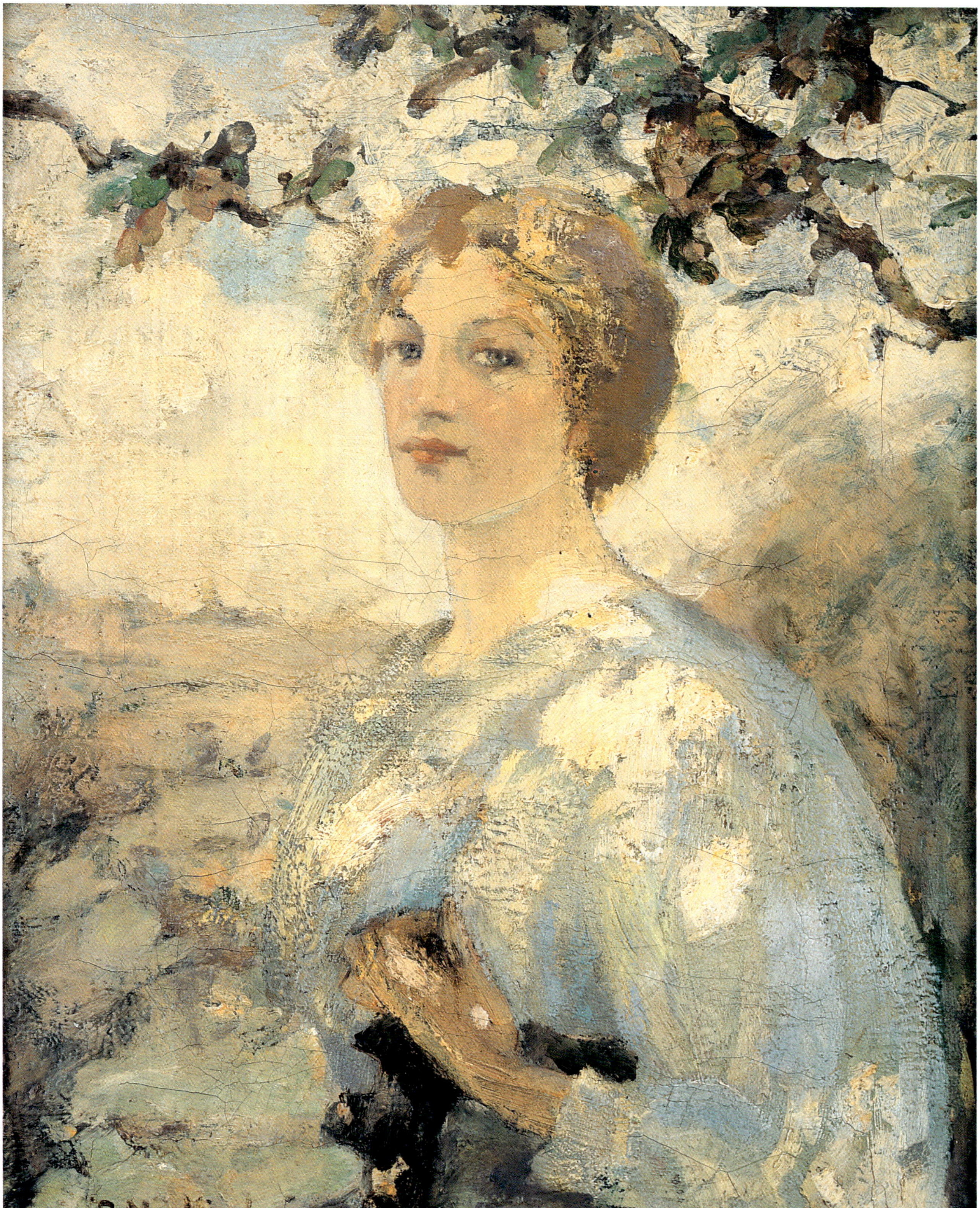

> the right is purple, beautiful as the depth of foxglove bells, a delicate and yet a full sensation of the beauty of modern life from which all grossness has been omitted.[3]

Guthrie submitted *Midsummer* as his Diploma Work when he was elected full Academician of the Royal Scottish Academy in 1892. According to his biographer Sir James L. Caw, Guthrie later regretted his choice. By then he was well-known for his portraits, but we can only regret that he did not paint more works like *Midsummer.* Clearly the work was well thought of at the time, because it was lent by the Royal Scottish Academy to the Glasgow Institute for its 1895 exhibition.

David Gauld, one of the most innovative of the Glasgow Boys in his younger days, also used this sunlight effect in portraits of young girls under shady trees, paintings which were wrongly labelled 'impressionist' (as indeed was *Midsummer*). Gauld painted these portraits with a sunlit background, and in the very charming *Head of a Girl* sunlight encircles her head, one cheek and the front of her blouse. In *Portrait* (pl.15) this effect can be seen round the pert little hat, neck, collar and shoulders. The model in both these paintings may well be Margaret Paterson, who became Gauld's wife in 1893. Artistically it is a very daring exercise, as the tonal contrasts between sun and shade can destroy the feeling of form, but it was one which Bessie MacNicol explored in her own way to great effect. In her paintings the figure is sometimes set against a distant landscape, as in *Under the Apple Tree* and *Apple Blossom.*

In *Under the Apple Tree* she painted sunlight shining through foliage on to the girl's hair and cheek and in patches on her white blouse. Possibly through alterations made after 1896 this work has become much more than a portrait. Every brush stroke contributes to its design and realisation as a considerable picture. It satisfies the eye by the balance of tone and colour as well as its happy description of a pretty young girl, who resembles an Italian Quattrocento angel, against a sunlit landscape. The picture is a celebration of summer, of youth, of life and of hope.

The mirror is a curious piece of sophistication in an open air painting, unless it was placed for purely pictorial reasons to reflect the light. Possibly it may have been a later addition, as it does not appear in the portrait study already mentioned. Woman with mirror is a recurring subject in art, more usually associated with the female nude as Venus, seen in paintings of the Venetian School by Giovanni Bellini and Titian and, in a painting more familiar to the British public, the 'Rokeby' Venus. *The Toilet of Venus* by Diego Velasquez is in the National Gallery in London, and Bessie MacNicol was to tackle a large painting of this subject at a later date with *Vanity.*

Ein schottisches Mädchen and *The Green Hat*

Bessie MacNicol first exhibited abroad in 1895 at the Glaspalast in Munich. The following year she sent a three-quarter length portrait of her younger

PLATE 15
DAVID GAULD
Portrait
Oil on canvas
19¾x16
Lord and Lady Macfarlane of Bearsden
(photo: The Fine Art Society)

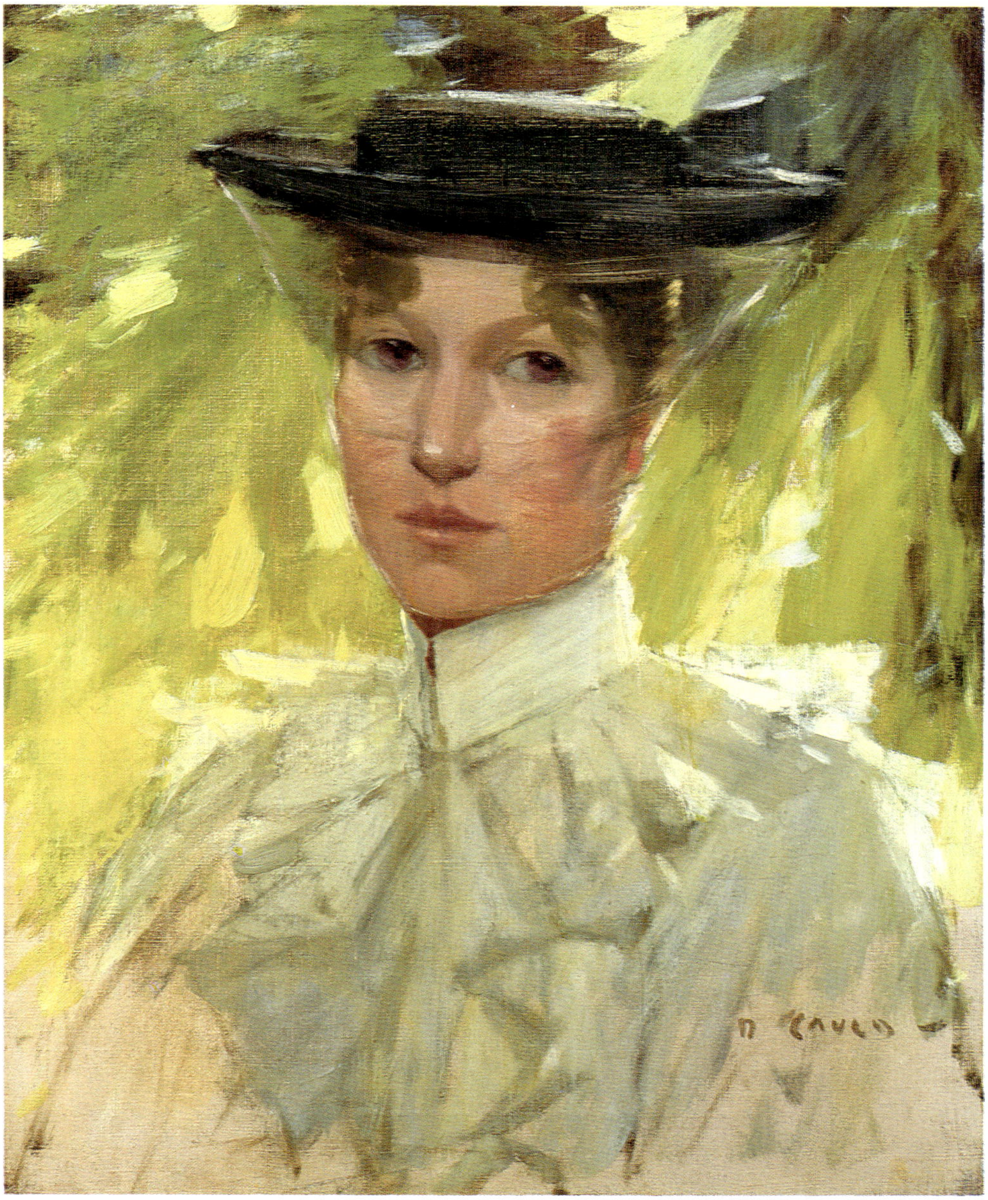

sister Jessie to the exhibition of the Munich Secession (Internationale Kunstausstellung). It was titled *Ein schottisches Mädchen* (pl.17) and is illustrated in the catalogue. This painting has not been traced, but it would seem that for some reason she may have altered it at a later date, adding green material to the hat and cutting the canvas down drastically, so that now it depicts only the head and shoulders. It is probable that this is the painting *The Green Hat* (pl.16) in the City of Edinburgh Collection. What is even more interesting is that the marked resemblance to her sister Jessie has gone, as if that no longer mattered. The same thing may have happened to *Under the Apple Tree*, which could have started as a straightforward portrait, but

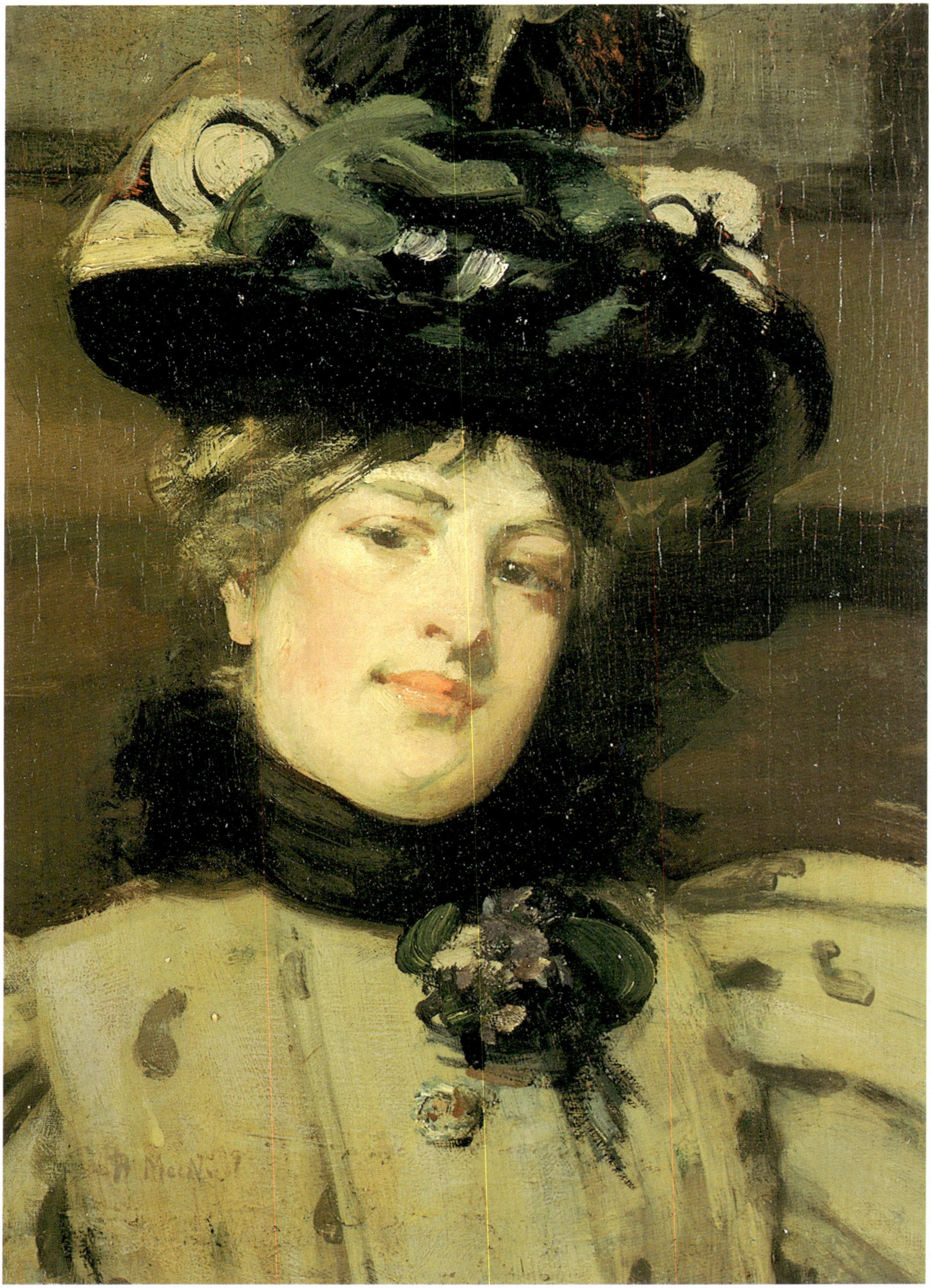

later was transformed to a more universal statement, speaking to everyone in painterly terms. This kind of portrait, which was not so dependent on likeness to the sitter, was called at that time a fancy portrait.

There is reason to suppose that Jessie MacNicol was at Kirkcudbright along with her sister in 1896, possibly as chaperone. At the top of the first letter to Hornel written on 9th December, 1896 is a note 'Miss Little MacN and Miss Unknown MacN send greetings' which suggests an earlier acquaintance. Jessie was shorter than her sister Minnie.[5]

1 Letter from George Henry to E. A. Hornel 1/15, Broughton House, Kirkcudbright
2 *The Studio* vol.XXXVII 1904 p.206
3 George Moore, *Modern Painting*, new edition 1897 p.206
4 Sir James Caw, *Sir James Guthrie: A Biography* 1932 p.58
5 Bessie MacNicol letter no.1, Broughton House, Kirkcudbright

(opposite)
PLATE 16
The Green Hat
Oil on canvas
20¼x14
The City Art Centre, Edinburgh

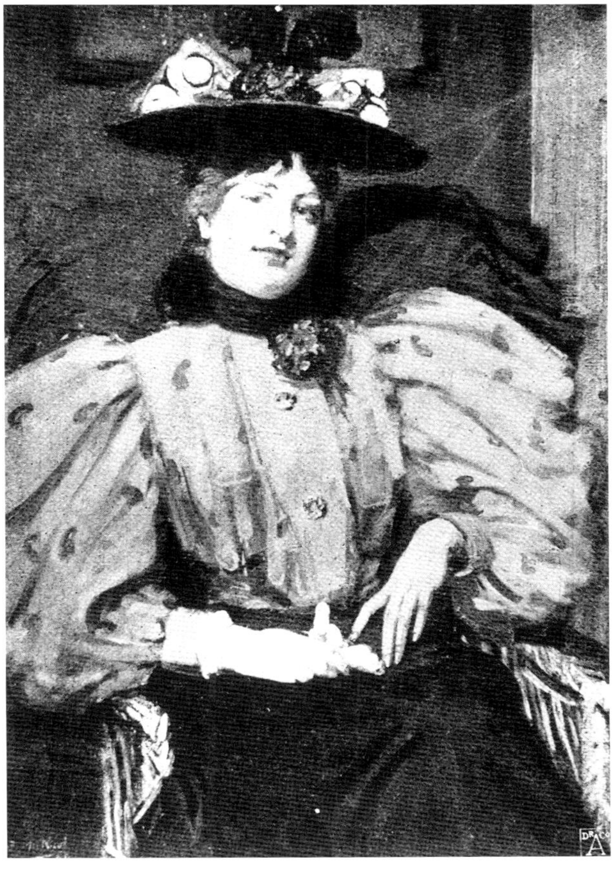

PLATE 17
Ein schottisches Mädchen
Illustration in Exhibition Catalogue, Munich Secession 1896

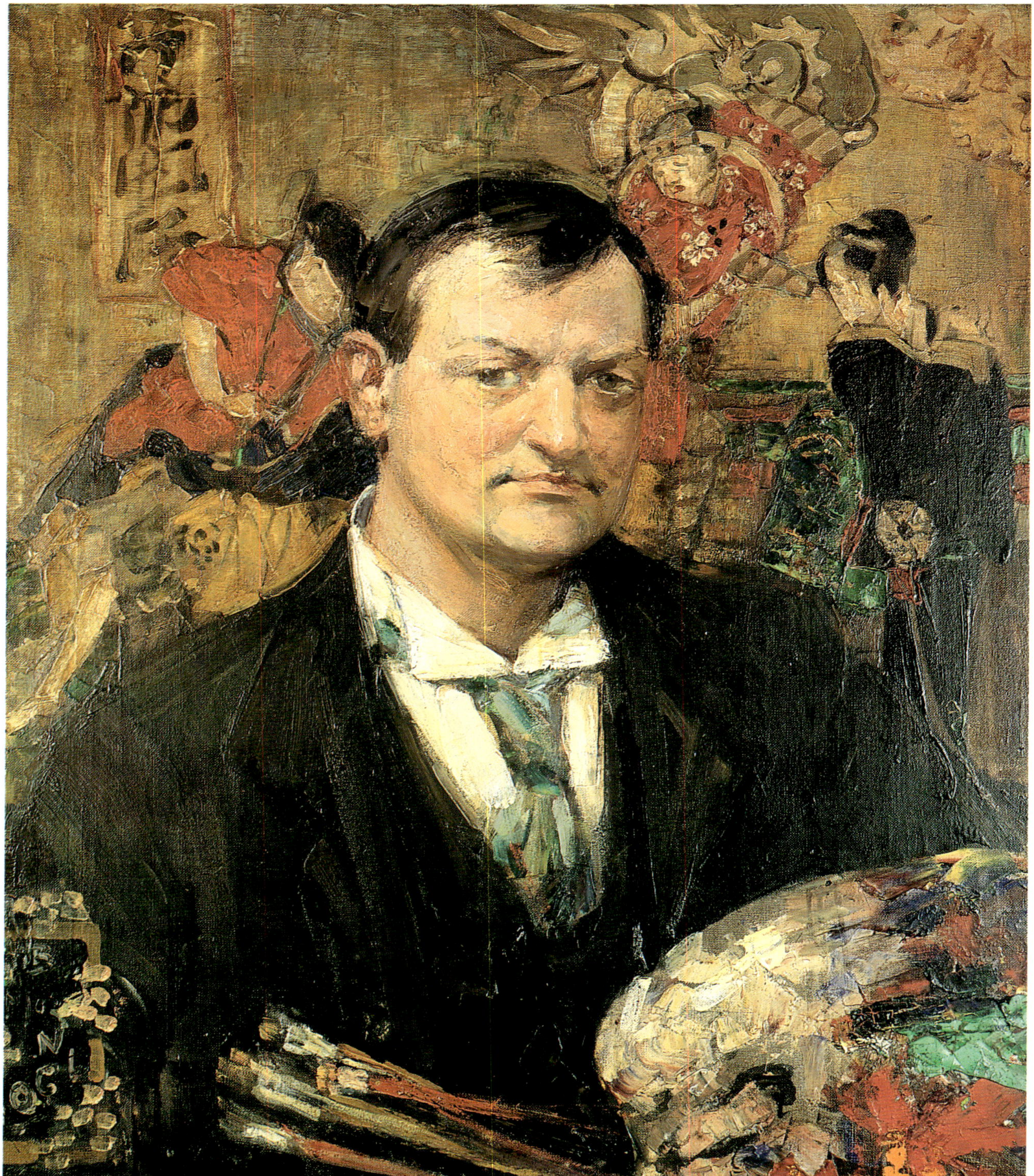

6. PORTRAIT OF E. A. HORNEL

We are on firmer ground from December 1896 with the help of the nine letters which were written from then until Christmas 1897 to 'My Dear Ned' and usually ending 'Yours, B. MacNicol'. This was the form of her name which she preferred to use professionally to sign her paintings. Later this preference was published in *The Scots Pictorial*:

> Mrs. Frew prefers to be known in the world of art as B. MacNicol – it might be Benjamin or Barney and it need not necessarily be Bessie. She is bon camarade, and can talk art with the best of the mere male painters.[1]

Many of the letters contain references to the portrait of Hornel (pl.18) painted by Bessie MacNicol in his studio in Kirkcudbright's High Street, about its frame, what the other Glasgow Boys thought of it, and about a possible exchange of paintings arranged between them. The portrait now hangs in the dining-room of Broughton House, but there is no firm evidence about which painting she received in return.

In 1896 Hornel was still painting Japanese pictures, probably because of the success of his 1895 exhibition. He had brought back from Japan kimonos and robes and a Japanese wall hanging. In the portrait he is seen in front of this hanging, palette and brushes in hand, as if he were about to paint. The picture is signed at the lower left in a pseudo-oriental vertical manner, which is not very convincing and looks like a high spirited gesture. The Japanese figures of the hanging have been rearranged by the artist for her own purposes, and the rich red colours are echoed in the red paint on his palette. We know what changes she made, because there is a contemporary photograph of Hornel (pl.22) in front of the same hanging taken by his friend Robert McConchie, a fine photographer who has left a fascinating record of Kirkcudbright at this time. We can see also that the likeness obtained by Bessie MacNicol is excellent. Here is Hornel – still youthful at thirty-two – straightforwardly and strongly painted, refuting completely all the stupid and hurting criticisms that appeared in the press when it was exhibited at the Glasgow Institute in 1897. No wonder Hornel was happy to receive the painting and hang it in his own home.

(opposite)
PLATE 18
E. A. Hornel
Oil on canvas
30x24
The National Trust for Scotland, Broughton House

To begin with most reviewers agreed that it was not a good likeness. *The Kirkcudbrightshire Advertiser* commented:

> . . . Miss Bessie MacNicol has a vigorously executed portrait of the artist hung in the third gallery. The workmanship is thoroughly creditable, but the likeness is not by any means flattering to Mr. Hornel.[2]

Megilp in the weekly periodical *The Bailie* wrote:

> . . . A portrait that will arouse not a little controversy is one that Miss Bessie M'Nicol has sent to the Exhibition. It is a likeness of E. A. Hornel, who is represented with palette and brushes in his hands. The head is seen against a background of Japanese figures and designs. While the work has many strong points of colour and handling, the likeness ——.[3]

A well-known local painter, who has not been identified, sprang to her defence. He is quoted in *The Bailie* the following week as saying 'The likeness has been commented on by many artists who know Hornel as being quite remarkable.'[4] A cartoon of the picture appeared in *Quiz* with a caption underneath reading 'Fancy portrait of a bruiser'.[5] A week later in a concluding article the reviewer noted 'Bessie MacNicol's portrait of E. A. Hornel (456) is good, but the artist might have saved a little paint, some of which is just a wee bit too prominent.'[6]

It was the *Glasgow Herald* which had the most comment, although reserved for the final review, when it was the last picture to be mentioned. Consequently it was not criticised with other portraits, but with figure compositions and genre works. Obviously the critic did not know how to treat this portrait. He must have thought it was a presumptious work by a lady artist and not to be taken seriously, writing:

> . . . Bessie MacNicol's bust portrait of E. A. Hornel (no. 456) is strongly painted and at least up to a point it is characteristic. The artist sits in his studio, his palette glowing with pigments. Behind him are a couple of Japanese elves, whispering as it seems in his ear. Either their suggestions are unwelcome, or Mr Hornel has grown impatient of sitting, for the expression of his face, Napoleonic in its strength, the forelock carried down the ample brow, is not that of a meek and saintly colourist. Probably Mr. Hornel would make reply that he does not wish to pose in such a role. What we feel is that the lady artist, seeking to reveal the strength of her brother artist, has not sufficiently interpreted the bright intelligence with which he is not less assuredly endowed.[7]

That facetious and insulting criticism shows the bias with which this *lady* artist was treated. She must have particularly resented the term 'lady artist' as she had chosen not to join the Lady Artists' Club in Blythswood Square.[8]

Edward Atkinson Hornel

In 1896 Hornel was thirty-two years of age. He had been born at Bacchus Marsh, Victoria on 17th July 1864, the younger of twin sons born to William Lidderdale Hornell and his wife Anne Elizabeth Habbishaw. His parents had emigrated to Australia in 1860, but returned to Scotland and to Kirkcudbright in 1866. It was by a twist of fate that Hornel became a painter, for after he had finished his schooling and was going out to Australia to become a farmer, news came that his father, who had returned to Australia, had died at Coimadia, Victoria on 19th June 1879. It was only then that he decided to go to Edinburgh to study painting at the Trustees

Academy, later continuing his studies in Antwerp under Charles Verlat. He returned to Kirkcudbright in 1885 and by 1896 had established himself as one of the most important younger Glasgow Boys. He stayed most of the year in Kirkcudbright, but rented a studio in Glasgow to finish and prepare work for the Institute exhibition, which opened at that time at the Fine Art Institute in early February. Before 1897 George Henry had helped Hornel to find studio accommodation in Glasgow. In return Hornel or his sisters found lodgings for the summer visitors to Kirkcudbright. In 1897, however, Hornel does not seem to have gone to Glasgow until the end of February, perhaps because his portrait – painted by a *woman* – was hanging in the exhibition and he expected ribbing from fellow artists.

1 *The Scots Pictorial* 5 April 1902
2 *The Kirkcudbrightshire Advertiser* 12 February 1897
3 *The Bailie* 20 January 1897 p.12
4 *The Bailie* 27 January 1897 p.7
5 *Quiz* 11 February 1897 p.92
6 *Quiz* 18 February 1897 p.108
7 *Glasgow Herald* 11 March 1897
8 As the records of the Glasgow Society of Lady Artists were lost in a fire in 1901, it is not possible to confirm or deny that Bessie MacNicol was a member. The Society was founded in 1882 and played an important part in giving women a centre for exhibiting paintings and craftwork and a congenial social meeting place. It had expanded into a residential Club with handsome premises at 5 Blythswood Square by 1896. Bessie MacNicol may well have participated in the Fancy Fayre *Tableaux Vivants* for which Alexander Frew lent costumes in 1895. As a confirmed painter in oils it is quite likely that she would not have had so much in common with artist designers, but most of her contemporaries were members, including Annie Rose Laing, although the latter was not elected until 1908. In 1903 *The Studio* noted 'There is much good work, however, done by lady painters in Glasgow who do not exhibit at the Ladies Club. Miss Bessie MacNicol was recently seen in great strength at a small exhibition of a new society, where several portraits, and a very strong study of the nude, showed that she is possessed of great power.' (*The Studio* vol.XXVIII 1903 *Studio Talk: Glasgow* p.137)

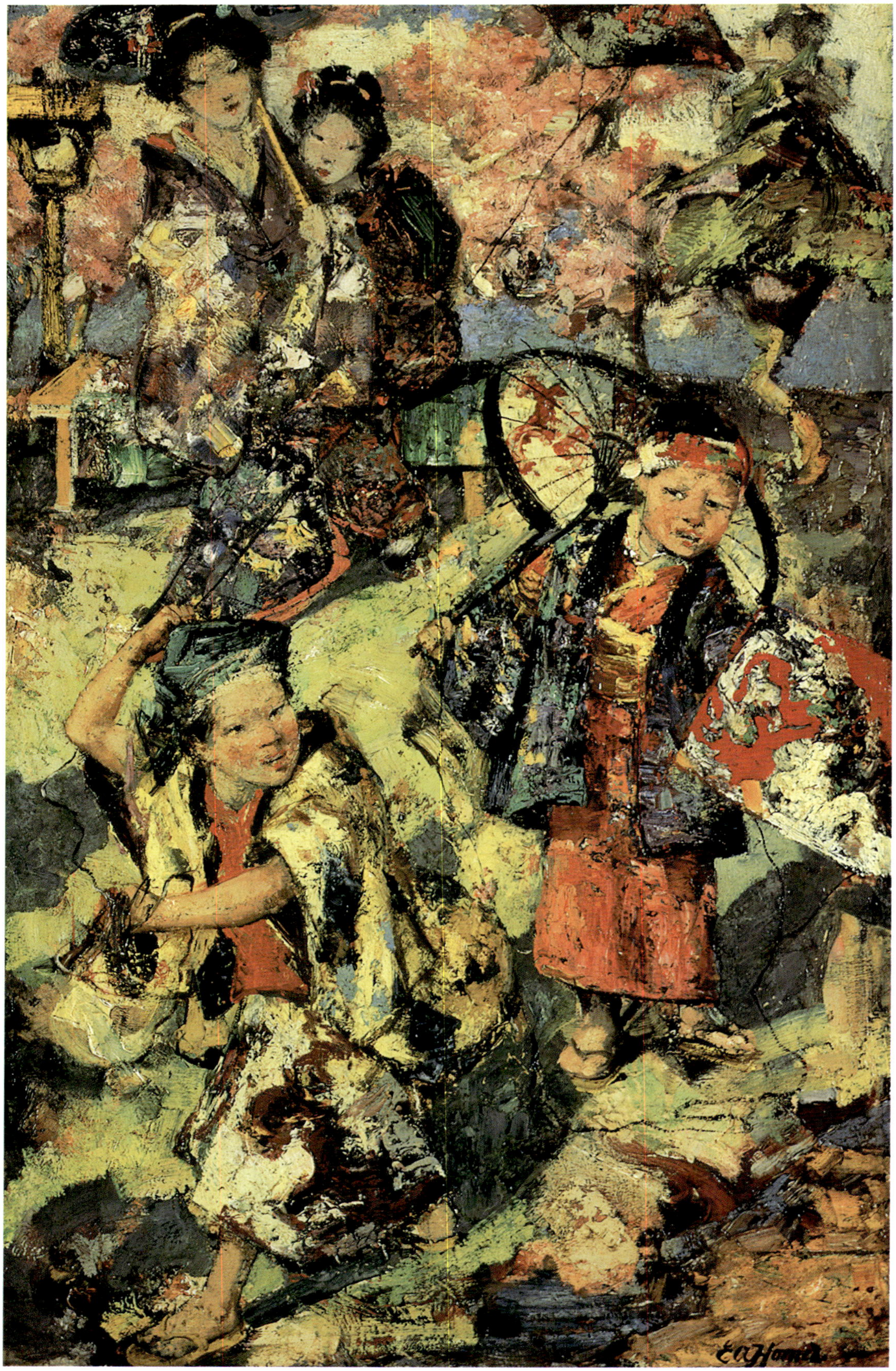

7. 1897

It is uncertain where Bessie MacNicol and possibly her sister stayed in Kirkcudbright, but her letters to Hornel end always with greetings to 'Missie'. Certainly this person stayed with the MacNicols at 4 Oakfield Terrace in February 1897, when 'Missie' and Hornel came to Glasgow. After their visit Bessie wrote in a letter to Hornel:

> . . . I am sorry Missie has been so bad – your people will be thinking Glasgow does not agree with her. It gave you a wee turn of attending on her after she had attended so much on you. Splendid training!

'Missie' may have been a pet name for one of Hornel's sisters. His eldest sister was Margaret, who was by then married to William Mouncey, a painter and decorator in Kirkcudbright before becoming a full-time landscape painter in 1886. However 'Missie' does not sound right for a married woman. It seems much more likely that Bessie MacNicol was referring to Elizabeth Hornel, two years younger than Margaret. Known as 'Tizzy' to her family, Elizabeth Hornel was always referred to as *Miss* Hornel, as was the custom then when addressing the eldest unmarried daughter in a family. Tizzy kept house for her brother, first in the former Custom House in the High Street opposite the family home and then when he moved in 1901 to Broughton House, a handsome Georgian house behind a raised forecourt in the same street.[1]

Personality of Bessie MacNicol

The nine letters give the only clues we have to the personality of Bessie MacNicol and only at this one period of her life, when she was about twenty-eight years of age. In them she appears fun-loving, full of life and high spirits, but at the same time having a deep commitment to painting. A happy home life is hinted at with her father, now Headmaster of Overnewton School, her English mother and two younger sisters. With them she was a *New Woman* of the time, revelling in new-found if not complete emancipation. She had many friends, both men and women, and enjoyed visits to the theatre and many other 'sprees'. In December 1896 she went to a Fancy Dress Ball at the St. Andrew's Hall in aid of the Scottish Artists' Benevolent Fund. Her partner was Alexander Frew, dark-haired and handsome, a one-time doctor of medicine, now a full-time painter, whom she was to marry in 1899. She gave a graphic description of this entertainment to Hornel. The Ball was run on the same lines as the famous Costume Ball of 1889. Alexander Frew as Antonello da Messina was wearing the same dramatic Florentine costume with yellow and

(opposite)
PLATE 19
E. A. Hornel
Kite-Flying, Japan
Oil on canvas
30x19
National Galleries of Scotland

black striped hose which had been captured in pastel at the 1889 Ball by James Paterson (pl.20), as well as in an oil study by Peter Macgregor Wilson (pl.21). Apparently artists were ready at their easels at the 1896 Ball – as in 1889 – to paint guests in costume, but because no souvenir album was published the results have not come to light.

There are descriptions of visits to the theatre with friends. Harry Spence, 'the Josser', is mentioned in the third letter:

> Harry is holding receptions & private views just now in his studio so I have not seen him since we were at the pantomime. I was there again last night, & at the 'Shop Girl' last week. I have many prospective sprees of the same kind so I am gay enough. William Guthrie & wife take me sometimes – he says I am not to go with 'worthless young men.'[2]

In 1897 the latest craze was cycling, for women as well as for men. In her sixth letter she wrote:

> John Keppie came up to see me the day after I returned from Kirkcudbright, & was inviting me to go for a cycle run with him. I have got a new kind of cycling skirt, which is divided, so far up, but is just like a walking skirt when I am standing. I put the Mater into fits when I was in the shop buying it, by dancing a hornpipe behind the woman's back. They are wide Jack Tar bags! I am getting on splendidly & am quite a scorcher. I have not gone more than 10 miles yet but can pass machines & people without running them down for certain.

However the open air and the countryside held drawbacks to pleasure for Bessie MacNicol. We learn from her letters that she was a martyr to hay

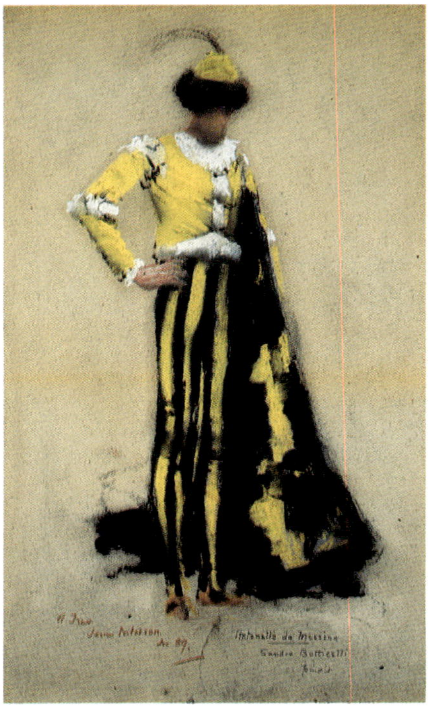

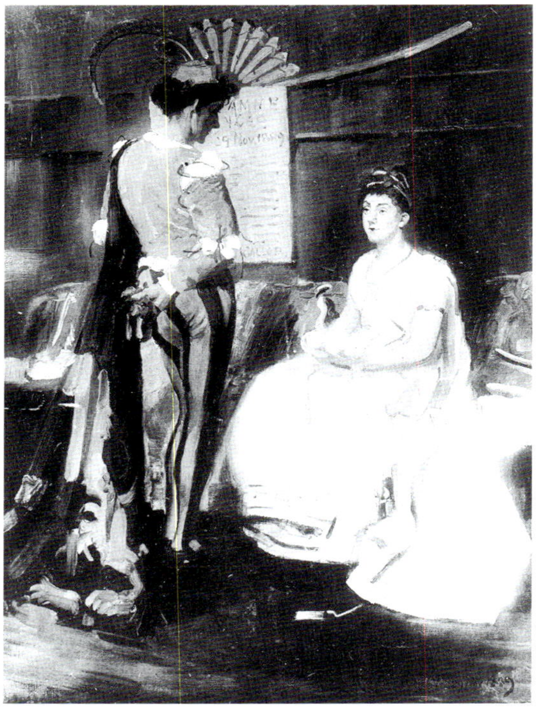

(left)
PLATE 20
JAMES PATERSON
Alexander Frew as Antonello da Messina
Pastel
Private collection
(photo:R.M.Muirhead)

(right)
PLATE 21
PETER MACGREGOR WILSON
Alexander Frew at the Costume Ball 1889
Untraced
(photo:City of Glasgow Libraries & Archives, Mitchell Library)

fever. Summer was for her a time of misery. Describing a journey back to Glasgow from Dumfries she wrote:

> . . . We did not have our engaged compartment after all – such crowds of people – a 'creature' came in at Dumfries, with a big bunch of flowers – & I was liquid all the way to Kilmarnock.

Again writing of a proposed holiday at Ardrishaig in July:

> Our people talk of going to Ardrishaig at once – so I expect there will, ere long, be nothing left of me but my boots – hay-fever will have melted me.[3]

Comments on Painting and Painters

While enjoying life in the company of friends, Bessie MacNicol was a fully committed professional painter and this comes through in her letters to Hornel. In her second letter to him she discusses the use of colours:

> I wanted to tell you also something about paint – Frew told me, & whatever he may not know I think he does know something of the chemistry of colours. He says chromes can stand any length of time without being affected by the air, as there is so much sulphur in both, but used in conjunction with lead [Flake White] it turns black in a few days. Also that chromes used with Cadmium turns black almost at once – Emerald green also – even used pure. When he said this I remembered your see-saw picture[4] – how 3 times you had 'brought it up' & each time I had thought it impossible to do so. I am using Zinc White now myself – & Cadmium in flesh painting.

At the end of this letter Bessie MacNicol adds:

> I have been using a new Crimson – said to be absolutely permanent – Alizarin Crimson – of same colour & consistency as crimson lake. Alizarin Scarlet can also be had though I have not seen it.

Bessie MacNicol had rented a studio at 175 St. Vincent Street (pl.23) since 1893, which she used until her marriage in 1899. In her fifth letter she describes going back to it, probably in May, after a visit to Kirkcudbright:

> I went to the Studio yesterday, & my heart turned sick at the grime not to talk of White Elephants in the way of unsold pics.

She writes of an interesting encounter with her old Headmaster Fra Newbery:

> Poor old Newbery is complaining bitterly about all the best men leaving Glasgow – 'Johnny [Lavery] is gone & won't come back I'm sure . . . Jamie [Guthrie] has the idea in the balance . . . Teddy [Walton] has gone & is doing well.' I sympathised with him & thought to ask him if he felt lonely here, but thought it might pass for 'MacNicol cheek'. He has some good work – with more distinction than anything he has done. I asked him if he was going to send 2 to the Institute. 'Oh I don't know – there is still a good deal of bad feeling in Glasgow – I am still looked on as too much of a damned Englishman!' I said 'The best men do not think so?' 'Oh no – just the 'moles' but they have some power!!'[5]

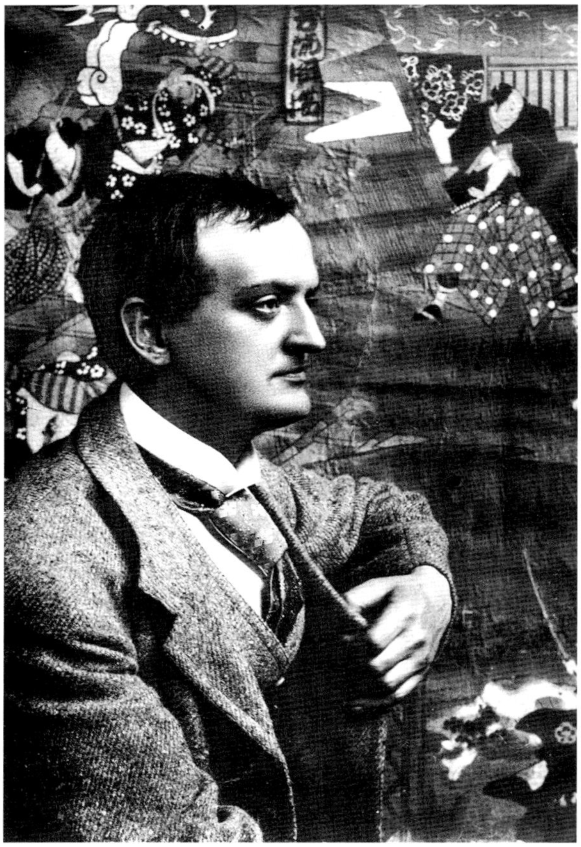

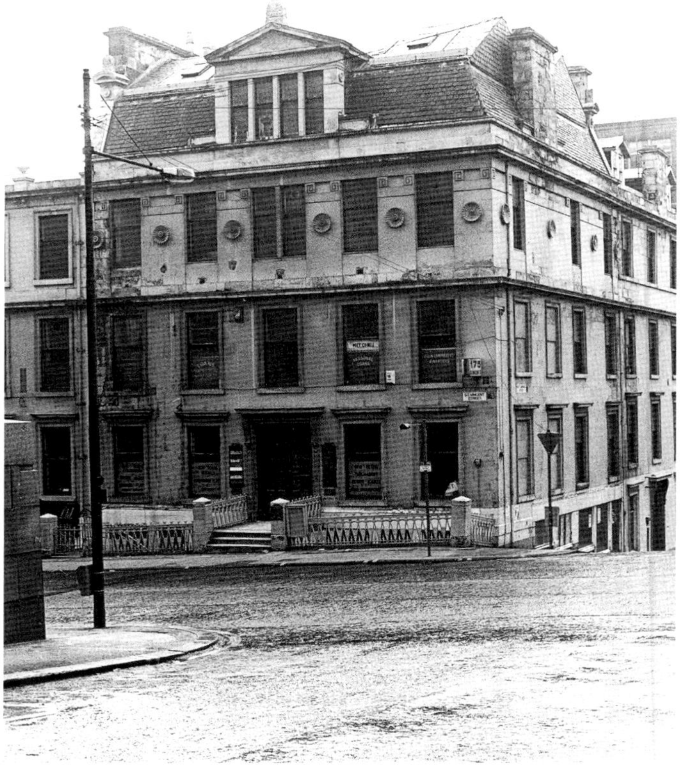

(left)
PLATE 22
E. A. Hornel
Photograph by
Robert McConchie
The Stewartry Museum,
Kirkcudbright

(right)
PLATE 23
175 St Vincent Street, Glasgow
(photo:James Cunningham)

EXCHANGE OF PAINTINGS?

The binding thread through all the letters is the portrait of Hornel, which he must have expressed a wish to own. She discusses a frame for it and before the Institute exhibition gives the reactions of other painters in Glasgow to it. But what is even more interesting, if one reads between the lines, is that she gives hints that an exchange of paintings took place.

In the second letter she writes:

> About my frame for your portrait – perhaps it will do for the Institute, & then you can please yourself afterwards if you still care to have the picture, old boy – Have you a photo of yourself – if so – send me one – like a dear!

A photograph must have been sent, for she is worried that Hornel has put on weight and begs him not to eat so much or drink so much beer until he comes to town '. . . or the boys will be saying my portrait of you is so emaciated.'

In the fourth letter Bessie MacNicol is depressed because she is trying to finish a portrait that is proving difficult and doubts whether she will be able to go to Kirkcudbright in May. There is a hint of a possible exchange of paintings:

> . . . I am going to remind you that you once said you would do a wee fan-dango for me – a fantasy in paint! E. A. Hornel Esq. or something else. If it is to bother you of course, it does not matter a hang.

The visit to Kirkcudbright took place after all. The arrangement must have been discussed, because in June, a week before Queen Victoria's Diamond Jubilee, she wrote again:

> . . . If you are going to give me the Kite-flyer picture, Ned, don't you think a black frame would look jolly on it.

The 'Kite-flyer picture' may be the painting *Kite-flying, Japan* (pl.19), which is now in the National Galleries of Scotland. Bessie MacNicol had admired a Japanese picture by Hornel, which she had seen earlier at the Scottish Gallery in Edinburgh. She had called it a 'gem', so she was already interested in Hornel's richly painted evocations of Japanese life.[6]

Queen Victoria's Diamond Jubilee Celebrations

Bessie MacNicol spent the Jubilee weekend with friends, the Bells, at Monkton near Prestwick. On Jubilee Day 20th June 1897 they drove, cycled and rode to Ayr, where the flags and crowds so frightened the horses that they bolted, to the peril of the riders and a passing lady cyclist. Bessie MacNicol watched in horror as her friend Kate Bell was swung under her horse with her habit caught on the pommel until a passerby rescued her and she was able to remount. She wrote 'The fright drove away my hay fever for an hour.'[7]

In the same letter she is obviously concerned whether or not she is going to get her picture from Hornel, because she writes:

> We are going to Ardrishaig on Thursday – if you have not changed your mind about the pic. you might write about it like a good Christian man – whose promises hold good. I am having the black frame sorted for your portrait and will tell Menzies to send it on after I leave. How did your Jubilee get on – and were the Baloons [sic] a success?

Hornel was Convener of the Decorations Committee for Jubilee Day in Kirkcudbright. A quotation from *The Kirkcudbrightshire Advertiser* of 25 June 1897 answers her question:

> Evergreens in quantity were supplied from St. Mary's Isle and the Tolbooth, the Castle and the Public Buildings were soon a fluttering mass of parti coloured bunting and evergreen wreaths, while across the streets at every available point were strings of pennants, balloons and Chinese lanterns.

Perhaps it was the success of this undertaking which earned Hornel a place on Kirkcudbright Town Council, which he took up later in that year.

The Exchange Concluded

While at Ardrishaig, probably in early July, Bessie MacNicol at last received the letter from Hornel for which she was so anxiously waiting. She wrote in reply 'I see after all you are not a 'Sweep' but a God fearing keeper of promises!' For her own part of the bargain she now sent word to her framer 'to finish up the frame and send on the portrait at once . . . these expenses are mine Mr Hornel!'[8]

On her return to Glasgow from Ardrishaig she eventually did collect her painting, but not without difficulty as, understandably, Hornel's framer was not happy to hand the picture over without a warrant, in this case a letter sent by Hornel to his friend and fellow artist Thomas Corsan Morton. She was now happy and wrote:

> However I now have it and it looks tremendously fine. I am having an ivory cream frame on it as I do not like it so well when I tried it in a black one.[9]

The painting in the National Galleries of Scotland does not have a cream frame, but that might have been changed at a later date, when it was in the collection of Sir Hugh Reid Bart., who bequeathed the painting to the National Gallery on his death in 1934. There is no record of how he obtained the picture, but there is the interesting coincidence that he commissioned Bessie MacNicol to paint portraits of two of his sons in 1903. In addition he owned ten of her paintings, so he obviously knew and liked her work and possibly had seen Hornel's painting in her home. The portrait hangs above the mantelpiece in the dining room of Broughton House, but 'the Kite-flyer picture' was not listed in the sale of Alexander Frew's collection after his death in 1908, when several paintings by other Glasgow artists were sold by Robert McTear & Co. A painting *Kite-Flying, Japan* was sold in 1910 by the Glasgow dealer George Davidson in an exhibition of paintings by Hornel in his gallery in Sauchiehall Street. A critic in his review of the exhibition makes it clear that this was an earlier work of Hornel.[10] Perhaps Sir Hugh Reid purchased the picture at that exhibition, though it is still not clear how the painting had come back into Hornel's hands or perhaps to George Davidson.

The Last Letter

In her last letter, written before Christmas 1897, she seems to be much less lively than usual:

> . . . It is incredible how dull it is here – with fogs like midnight & not anything going on . . . I have been in bed for some weeks. Not that I seemed exactly ill but weak & useless. I went to the Dr. afterwards & he tested me in various ways & told me my internal organs were all out of order – & that it was a trouble of many years standing brought about by my liver – which is worthy of an 'old Indian' curry-flavoured! I am having a treatment of mercury & am already better than for years . . .[11]

Mercury has a depressive effect on the system, which may account for her next paragraph. After asking Hornel how he was getting on with his work, she wrote:

> . . . about mine I say nothing because you did not like it from the start. You should have told me that and not said you liked it very much – you sweep!

We have no means of knowing whether this was true or not, or whether she was suffering from a temporary bout of low spirits, for this is the last letter in the series. We must be grateful to Hornel for keeping these letters, along with all those he received from George Henry and several from other Glasgow artists. Regrettably there is no way of finding out whether her friendship with him continued or even if she returned to Kirkcudbright after 1897.

1 Bill Smith, *Hornel*, Atelier Books 1997 p.99
2 Bessie MacNicol letter no.3, Broughton House, Kirkcudbright
3 Ibid, letter no.5
4 Painting by Hornel *The See Saw* exh. RGIFA 1897 (98)
5 Bessie MacNicol letter no.3
6 Ibid, letter no.4
7 Ibid, letter no.6
8 Ibid, letter no.7
9 Ibid, letter no.8
10 *Glasgow Herald* 22 February 1910
11 Bessie MacNicol letter no.9

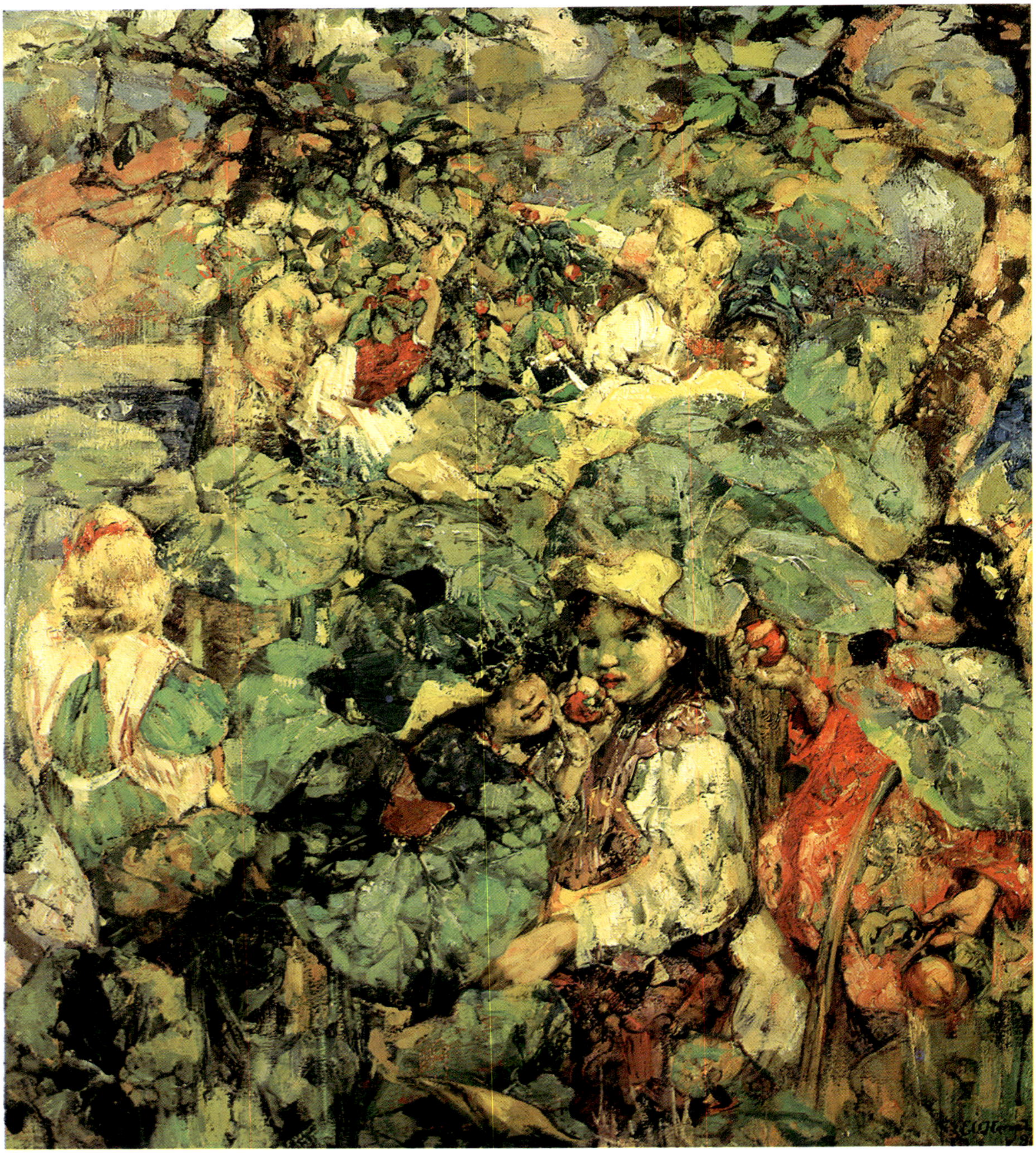

PLATE 24
E. A. HORNEL
In the Orchard
Oil on canvas
46x40
The City Art
Centre, Edinburgh

8. FRIENDSHIP BETWEEN HORNEL and MACNICOL

As far as her own work was concerned, her friendship with Hornel was the most important event of the years 1896 and 1897. Judging from the letters, the friendship was of a relaxed nature and she was not put off by his somewhat unbridled tongue. Writing of a conversation with Fra Newbery, she makes it into a dialogue:

> He asked me how I got on with you.
> 'Oh splendidly!! I admire him immensely, & there was nothing antagonistic in our natures.'
> 'Did he ever say naughty words?'
> 'Oh sometimes he said naughty cuss words, but I always tried to get one better.'
> He opened his eyes at my lie – or your powers![1]

The only reference to anything suggesting a romance between Hornel and her was the enquiry in her seventh letter:

> By the bye what do you mean by 'our gay festivities' that you spoke to Konky about? Do you mean our somnambulating walks to the Doachs? [Konky was Hornel's photographer friend Robert McConchie; the Doachs are wooden traps to catch salmon, which were about a mile further up the River Dee at Tongland]

Bessie MacNicol had to suffer at that time for her rash and unconventional association with Hornel. In her eighth letter she wrote:

> I have not yet done hearing of my terrible misdemeanours in working in your studio, Ned. If the people chaffed me I could take it, but it comes to pure scandal, or I should rather say not pure. One vile brute said he had the best authority for what he insinuated. In any case whenever I hear any man or woman has said anything or whenever they say anything to me, on my next meeting they are greeted with a strong British stare. It is not worth the fag of pretending even a nodding friendship after that . . . You see I do not care who knows the absolute truth but garbled accounts & added-to-stories are the devil's own work to combat.[2]

That is all the evidence we have now and it does not suggest any lasting attachment. They had many shared interests and had a common bond in both being twins. Hornel's twin brother William was then working in Sunderland, but Bessie's twin sister Mary had died when she was six years old. There had been another set of twins in each family, but they did not survive.

The letters are full of references to mutual friends and titbits of gossip from Glasgow. In her first letter she writes:

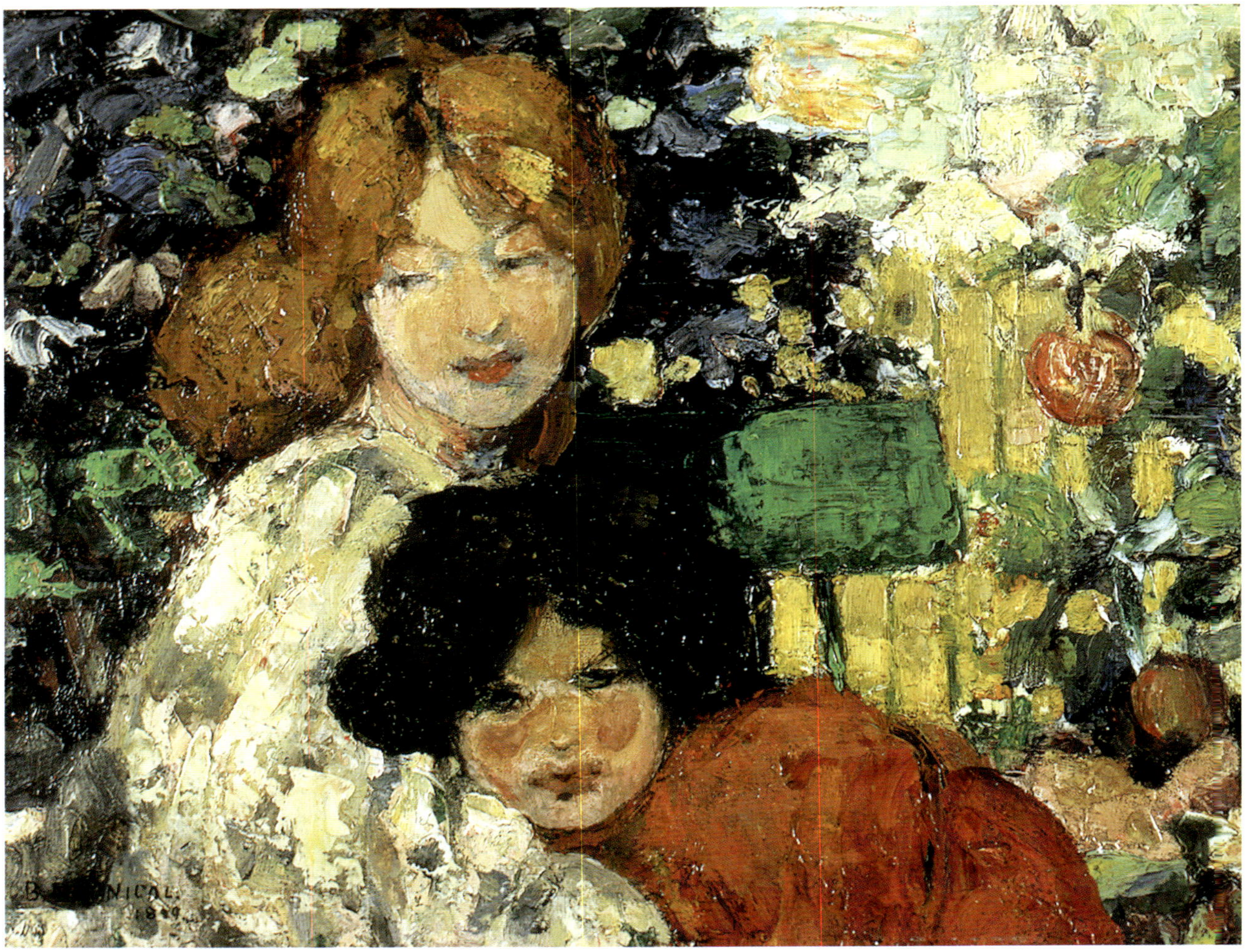

PLATE 25
Two Sisters
Oil on panel
11x14½
Ferens Art Gallery
Hull City Museums
& Art Galleries
(photo:Bridgeman Art
Library, London &
New York)

> I was hearing about Henry & it seems the men here say it would have been better if he had stayed a little longer with you, as he has gone back since he left your influence! How's that for High [Street]?

Later there is another snippet about him:

> The men say that Henry's work is commonplace. Henry and Grosvenor Thomas seem to be 'chers amis'. They always feed together.[3]

The male companion who would appear to have taken Henry's place as Hornel's 'cher ami' was a Canadian painter called Ivan Neilson. He is mentioned after the description in the second letter of a fire in Hornel's studio:

> The cooking of your 'gems' must have been a great scene. Grilled gems avec sauce de devilled cuss-words!! but I do hope they are not roasted to death. I think you should have let my Monticelli burn . . . Do you hear my Monticelli!!

Neilson is mentioned after this as the Canadian fire-eater, a reference that is obscure to us now, unless he helped to put out the fire. He is mentioned later in the third letter as 'the Enthusiast' painting at Glasgow School of Art with Newbery.

PLATE 26
Two Girls in a Garden
Oil on canvas
14x10
Private collection
(photo:R.M.Muirhead)

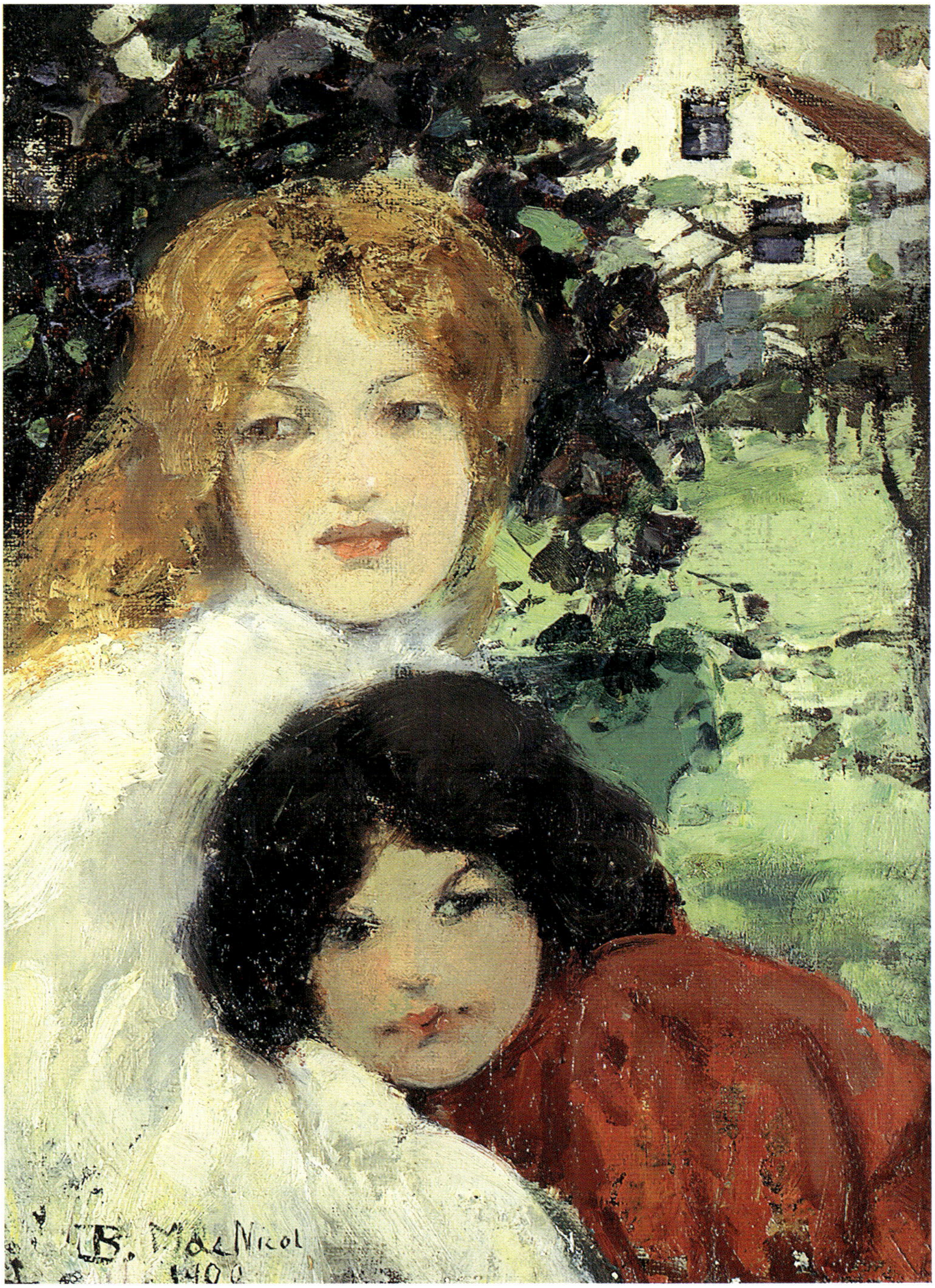

'MY MONTICELLI'

The paintings of the French painter Adolphe Monticelli exercised a strong influence on the work of Hornel and may also have influenced Bessie MacNicol. The 'gems' referred to may have been small paintings in the Japanese style, which Hornel was still painting after his return from Japan. 'My Monticelli' may perhaps refer to a small painting in the Ferens Art Gallery in Hull now called for no good reason *Two Sisters* (pl.25), depicting two small girls in a garden with the Kirkcudbright Tolbooth in the background. It must be one of the most richly coloured paintings she ever executed. It is painted with immense verve and *brio*, using rich impasto with brush and palette knife. This painting was most probably finished later from a sketch made in Kirkcudbright as it is dated 1899. The same subject was painted in 1900, titled more descriptively *Two Girls in a Garden* (pl.26). It is altogether a more sober painting and does not display the *bravura* and abandon of the smaller version.

Influence of Hornel

This brings one to the most important factor of Bessie MacNicol's friendship with Hornel: how much was she influenced by his painting? She reacted very strongly if anyone thought that Hornel had actually painted on her work. In her second letter a friend had reported that McOmish Dott, the dealer in Edinburgh to whom she had given a painting titled *Rose*, had said of it 'It is easily to be seen Hornel had most of the painting of that to do!' Her comment to that was 'I could of 'ker-slewed him when I heard.'

When one looks at her work before and after her stay in Kirkcudbright, his influence can be seen to be quite considerable. Her palette has lightened and brightened and there is more feeling of the open air and sunshine. However

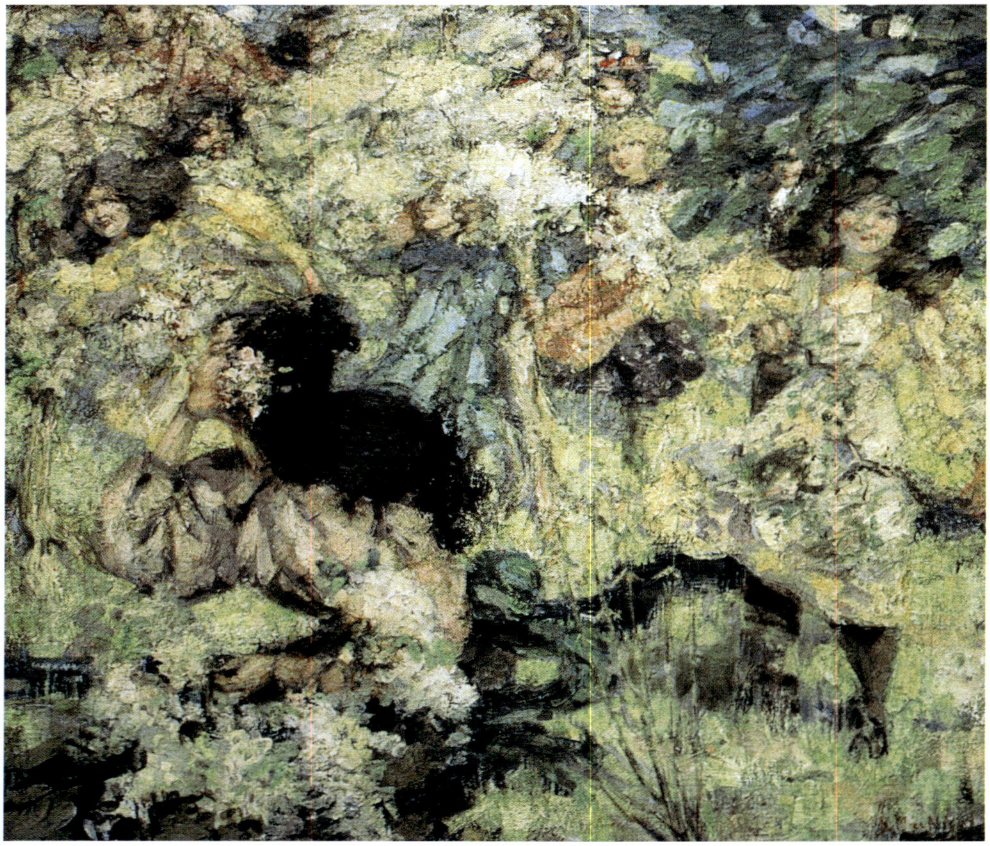

PLATE 27
A Battle of Flowers
Oil on canvas
Private collection
(photo:William Hardie Gallery)

this may be as much due to the environment at Kirkcudbright compared with dusty, smoky Glasgow. Her oil technique, always bold and broad, became more varied in the exploration of textures. Bessie MacNicol was obviously receptive to the work of other painters and readily admitted her admiration for Hornel's work. She was, however, no mere follower, but an artist in her own right. Her painting developed in its own way away from his influence.

Influence of Other Glasgow Painters

As we know so little of her own thoughts before the end of 1896, it is difficult to judge how much she owed to other Glasgow painters, for instance George Henry, and that is a pity as she probably owed a great deal to Henry. A painting by Bessie MacNicol, which was sent to the 3rd Biennale in Venice in 1899, was titled *A Battle of Flowers*. It may be – though there is no certainty – that an untitled work by her painted in 1897 is the same picture (pl.27). This is a strange and puzzling painting of a group of young girls – the number is even difficult to determine – who are running round with white blossoms, possibly lilac. This painting appears to be related to a work by Henry executed in 1895 called *Lilac*, which he exhibited at the Glasgow Institute in 1896. However in Bessie MacNicol's painting movement is more pronounced and she seems to be adding a great deal of her own to the interpretation of the subject. This must be one of her most ambitious and experimental works. George Henry must have painted *Lilac* in 1895 and this does suggest that Bessie MacNicol may have visited Kirkcudbright in that year. In paintings like *In the Orchard* (pl.24) and *The Dance of Spring* Hornel was also painting groups of children as early as 1891 and in 1892 he painted *Children at Play*. Hornel's *The Picnic* painted in 1893 has the same indeterminate number of children as Bessie MacNicol's *A Battle of Flowers*.[4]

Bessie MacNicol undoubtedly shared her love of painterly technique with many of the Glasgow Boys, as well as their love of the expressive possibilities of paint itself. To James Guthrie in particular she owed her interest in dappled sunlight in her paintings of young women in the open air under the foliage of trees. It was a theme she shared with another Glasgow Boy, David Gauld, who was a student at Glasgow School of Art when she was there. She may have met him again while painting in Kirkcudbright. In her third letter to Hornel she describes a visit to her studio from Gauld to see the portrait she had painted of Hornel:

> . . . He said he wished I had painted it in greys and purples. Also, wanted me to take out the palette & to paint the coat a grey black. Of course that is quite another story – at least Gauld's way of telling the same story.

Bessie MacNicol resisted this attempt to influence her against her own instinct. Though she was undoubtedly influenced by her fellow artists in her work, I think she always managed to follow her own intentions and tell her own story.

It is even more difficult to determine if Bessie MacNicol was either friendly with or influenced by other women painters working in Scotland. The women friends she mentions in her letters – Kate Bell and Jenny Blackwood Brown – were not painters, nor were her sisters Jessie and Minnie. She would certainly have known Katharine Cameron from student days at Glasgow School of Art and later in 1902, when Cameron exhibited with the Glasgow Society of Artists as Catherine Cameron, before deciding to change her name for professional reasons. In the second exhibition in 1903 Agnes Raeburn, Helen Paxton Brown, Janet Macdonald Aitken and Jessie M. King joined the exhibitors. The catalogue cover was designed by Jessie King (pl.50). As a painter in oils Bessie MacNicol would have less in common with artists interested in illustration. Though she loved flowers and often included them in her paintings, she never painted flowers by themselves like Katharine Cameron, nor did she master the art of etching.

The other women artists in the West of Scotland who were primarily painters in oil at that time were Stansmore Dean and Annie Rose Laing. Stansmore Dean painted portraits almost exclusively; although some were commissions, they were mainly of friends and relations. Annie Rose Laing specialised in urban interiors and portraits of beautiful women and children, which she painted with great skill but with little real inspiration. I feel that Bessie MacNicol found her own way forward and was more at home in the company of male artists. She was influenced by the Glasgow Boys and Whistler and by paintings of the old masters she had seen in the Louvre and the National Galleries in London and Edinburgh.

1 Bessie MacNicol letter no.3, Broughton House, Kirkcudbright
2 Ibid, letter no.8
3 Ibid, letter no.3
4 *The Picnic* is illustrated in *Hornel* by Bill Smith 1997 p.81

9. 1898

From 1898 until Bessie MacNicol's death in 1904 there are no letters or other primary sources of information other than her paintings and family photographs. Consequently it is a question of building upon what information can be gained from catalogues, printed reviews and art notes in periodicals.

AUTUMN

The First Exhibition of the International Society of Sculptors, Painters and Gravers was held in May 1898 at Knightsbridge in London. The President of the Society was James Abbott McNeill Whistler, an artist much admired by Glasgow painters. In this inaugural exhibition there were many works by Scottish artists, particularly from Glasgow. *The Scots Pictorial* noted 'The Scottish Lion is in fact rampant in this exhibition.'[1] Hung well and illustrated in the catalogue was a 'fancy portrait' by Bessie MacNicol titled *Autumn* (pl.28), now in Aberdeen Art Gallery. The starting off point for this painting may have been the Fancy Dress Ball held in the St. Andrews Hall in December 1896, which she attended with Alexander Frew. We do know that he owned a collection of costumes, some of which had been lent to the Fancy Fayre held by the Lady Artists' Club in the Fine Art Institute in 1895 and worn in *tableaux vivants*.[2] It may be that Bessie MacNicol went to the 1896 Fancy Dress Ball in one of these costumes and may have taken part in the *tableaux vivants* which were staged at that Ball. Her account of the Ball is in her first letter to Hornel, but unfortunately there is no detailed description of her dress. She wrote:

> The Ball has come & gone. I nearly 'corpsed' at it. To begin with my raving locks were hanging down my back – kept in place by an arrangement which was neither more nor less than an abridged halo . . . I went with Frew whose head was like Paderewski's 'gone black in a single night!!' He looked a villain of the deepest dye.

Photographs taken in 1897 by Alexander Frew are still in the possession of Bessie MacNicol's family. One of them shows her in fancy dress, a loose white blouse under a brocaded sleeveless top similar to that shown in *Autumn* (pl.29). She has an arrangement of fine metal chains keeping in place her long dark hair, which is hanging down her back. Could this be the dress that she wore at the Ball? The photograph is not at all flattering, but may have been used while painting the picture. As with *Under the Apple Tree*, what perhaps started out as a self-portrait in *Autumn* has become a totally convincing picture of a young girl posed against golden chestnut leaves with the sun filtering through foliage on to her cheek and blouse. The painting is masterly in its freedom of brushwork. Its colour is rich and harmonious. The subject of a woman personifying a season has been a favourite one with

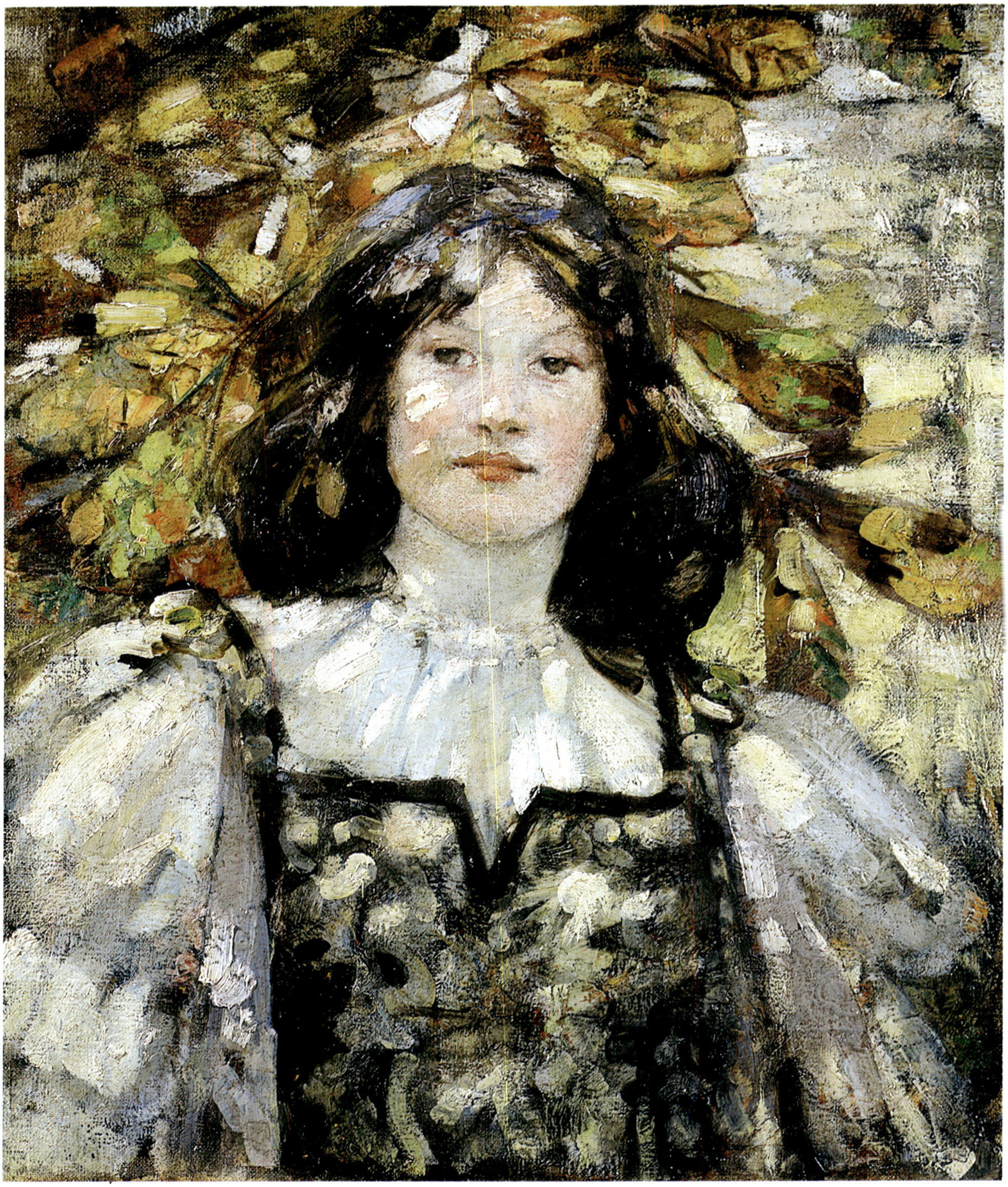

(opposite)
PLATE 28
Autumn
Oil on canvas
24x20
City of Aberdeen Art Gallery & Museums Collections

(right)
PLATE 29
Bessie MacNicol in 'Autumn' Dress
Photograph by
Alexander Frew

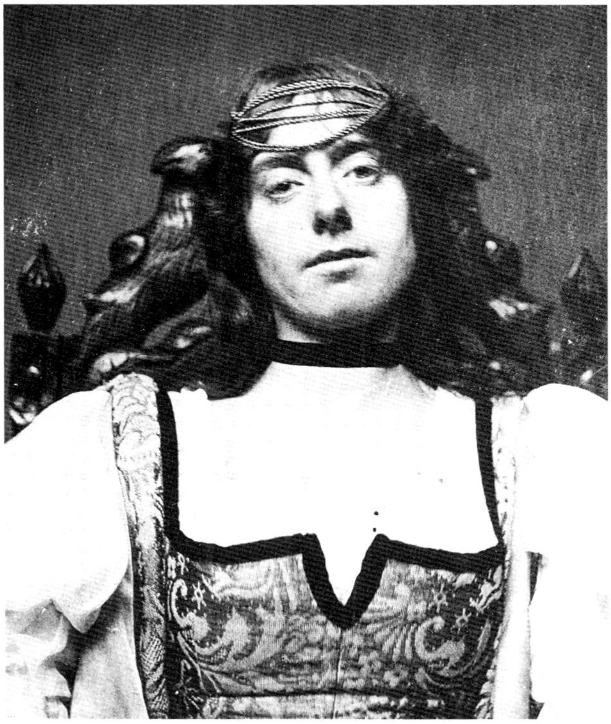

artists, but seldom can such a young face have been used to symbolise the mellow ageing of the year. Bessie MacNicol also executed the same year a smaller painting of a young girl's head titled *Spring* (pl.1), which does suggest more convincingly a fresh, youthful start to the year.

Tritomas

Tritomas (pl.30) is the title of a painting exhibited in 1898 at the IVth Vienna Secession Exhibition, but equally it might have been called *Summer*. Tritomas is the old botanical name for Kniphofias, flowers more familiarly known to us as 'Red Hot Pokers'. A girl is seen behind a screen of them and other flowers. Unfortunately this painting has not been traced and is known only from black and white reproductions. Without seeing the original, it is very difficult to make a judgement, as so much depends on colour in her paintings. It is to be hoped that this important work will one day come to light.

Although there is no evidence to link Bessie MacNicol with *The Immortals*, the members of the Charles Rennie Mackintosh circle, who met at *The Roaring Camp*, the name given to the two bungalows rented by John Keppie at Dunure, we do know that Keppie was already a cycling friend from her letters. In 1898 she painted a portrait of his sister Jessie, who was a member of the Mackintosh circle along with Agnes Raeburn, Janet Macdonald Aitken, Katharine Cameron and the Macdonald sisters, Margaret and Frances. Jessie's engagement to Charles Rennie Mackintosh had been broken off a few years earlier, when Mackintosh fell in love with Margaret Macdonald, and Jessie

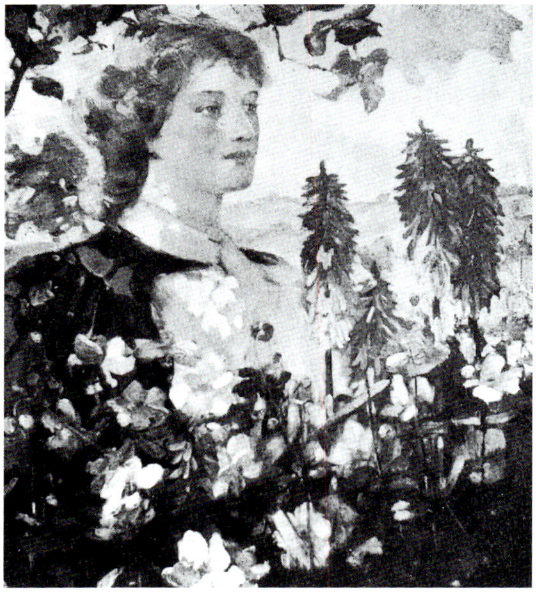

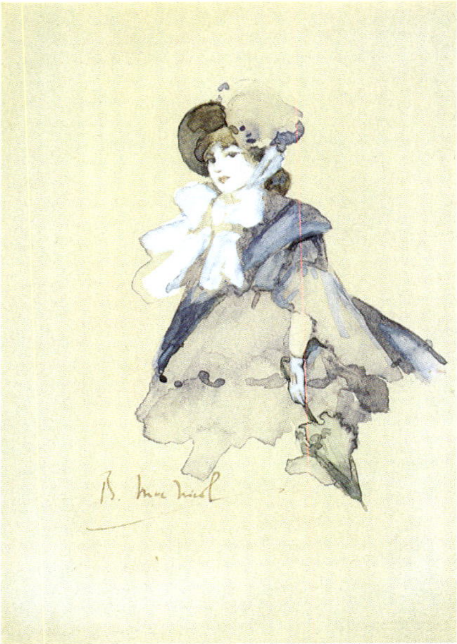

(left)
PLATE 30
Tritomas
Untraced
(photo:City of Glasgow Libraries & Archives, Mitchell Library)

(right)
PLATE 31
Girl in Blue with Parasol
Watercolour
Private collection
(photo:R.M.Muirhead)

never really recovered from that. Bessie MacNicol's portrait of her is quite straightforward and probably a very good likeness, but there was no attempt to do more than that. Jessie kept an Autograph Book in which she collected sketches and poems by her friends. These must have included both Bessie MacNicol and Alexander Frew, because in this album is a dainty jewel-like watercolour by Bessie MacNicol of a bonneted lady dressed in blue (pl.31) and a pen and ink sketch by Alexander Frew of Iona from the Ross of Mull. Jessie Keppie may possibly be associated with the painting *Tritomas*, for the girl bears a certain resemblance to the kindly face in the portrait of Jessie, and also to the girl in a later painting *In the Orchard* (pl.33), which once belonged to Hugh Hopkins, Jessie's cousin.

Exhibitions at Home and Abroad

The paintings of this period were well travelled, not only to exhibitions in other parts of the British Isles, but also to the Continent and to the United States. Bessie MacNicol exhibited in Glasgow of course and on several occasions at the Royal Scottish Academy in Edinburgh. She sent *Fifeshire Interior* to the Royal Academy in 1893, but it was the first and last time she exhibited there. She sent works to Liverpool and to Manchester as well as London.

On the Continent she exhibited regularly at the Glaspalast in Munich from 1895 to 1903. She sent two paintings to the Munich Secession Exhibition in 1896 and two to the IVth Secession Exhibition in Vienna in 1898. She exhibited in Ghent in the same year and sent a painting to the 3rd Biennale Fine Art Exhibition in Venice the following year. In 1904 she was exhibiting in an international exhibition at Düsseldorf. From 1896 to 1901 her work

(opposite left)
PLATE 32
Bessie MacNicol in the garden at 'Glendevon'
Photograph by Alexander Frew

(opposite right)
PLATE 33
In the Orchard
Oil on canvas
18x12
Private collection
(photo:R.M.Muirhead)

travelled across the Atlantic in company with other paintings from Glasgow to the St. Louis Exposition and to the Carnegie Institute in Pittsburgh. For the St Louis Exposition the paintings had to be submitted to a jury and several works by her were not accepted for exhibition.

One wonders about the condition of these paintings on their return to Glasgow. It may have been damage to the lower part of the canvas of *Ein schottisches Mädchen*, when it came back from the Munich Secession Exhibition in 1896, which forced Bessie MacNicol to cut the canvas to head and shoulders size.

Alexander Frew

Though there is no proof, it is very likely that Alexander Frew, who himself sent paintings abroad, may have helped Bessie exhibit overseas. Certainly it was he who arranged to send Glasgow works to St. Petersburg in 1898. They were friends by the end of 1896, if not earlier. In the summer of 1898 Bessie MacNicol must have been in Helensburgh often, because it was there she painted a portrait of him. Frew had owned a house in Helensburgh since 1894, principally because of his great interest in yachting. The house *Glendevon* is in William Street. Behind it is a little cottage with a north-facing window in the roof, which he used as a studio. It may be that Bessie MacNicol used this studio to paint his portrait. Another interest which was engrossing Frew at this time was photography. There are photographs taken by him of the garden at *Glendevon* in which Bessie MacNicol figures; in one she is holding a palette (pl.32). His sister Margaret, who may have stayed with him, married James Ewing Hunter, a Helensburgh doctor, the following year and there are

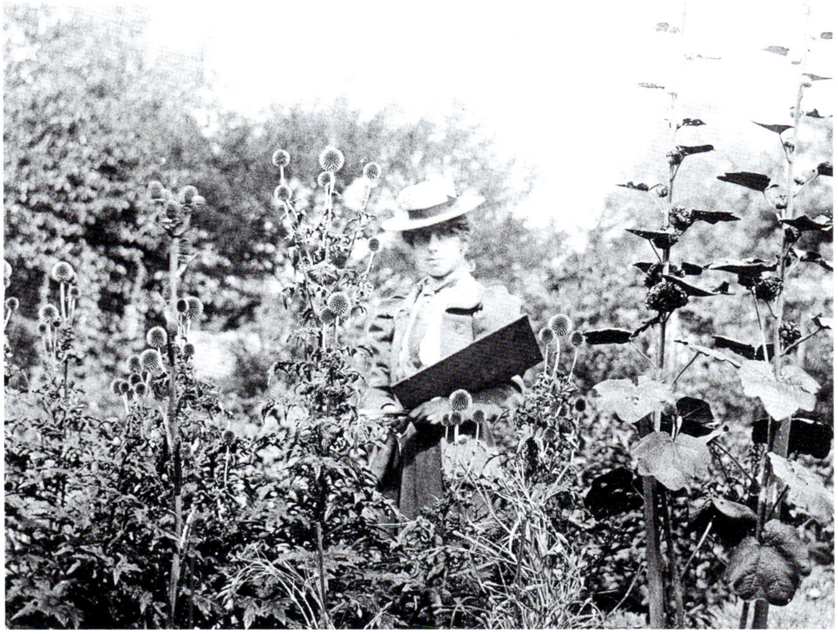

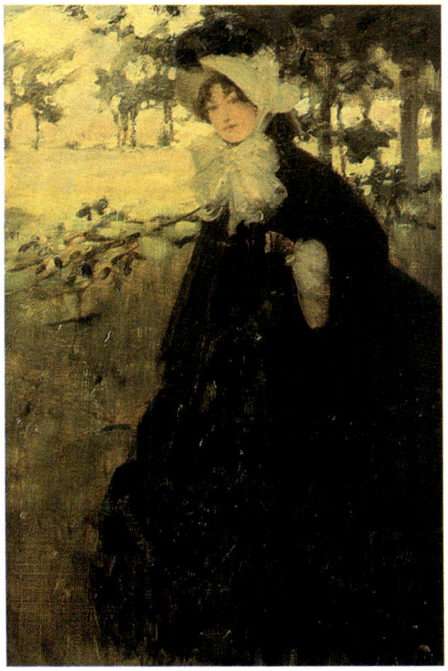

photographs of family groups which may include Frew's other sisters. Several of the photographs were taken in July 1897 at Ardrishaig, where the MacNicol family had been on holiday. Alexander Frew was a good photographer for his day and had an unconventional attitude to subject matter.

TRELAWNY OF THE WELLS

The other important event for Bessie MacNicol in 1898 was to see the play by Arthur Wing Pinero *Trelawny of the Wells*, either in London or when it came to Glasgow for six nights from 5th to 10th September. On September 7th *The Bailie* carried the following review:

> *Trelawny of the Wells* is being played at the Royalty with practically the same company as that when it was presented at the London Court Theatre . . . In dressing his play Mr. Pinero has gone to the old volumes of *Punch*. Crinolines, pork-pie hats, beaded nets for the hair, and elastic-sided boots set off the ladies, and show how crude, how tasteless, how uncomfortable, were our mid-Victorian costumes.

Bessie MacNicol did not share this critic's distaste for crinolines. Seeing this play with costumes after John Leech, the great *Punch* illustrator of the sixties, and the fine actress Irene Vanbrugh as Rose Trelawny, only confirmed her love of the period with the richness of its dresses, the frills and furbelows and

(below left)
PLATE 34
Trelawny of the Wells
S.Begg
The Illustrated London News 29 January 1898
(photo:City of Glasgow Libraries & Archives, Mitchell Library)

(below right)
PLATE 35
The Lace Cuff
Oil on canvas
26½x19½
Private collection

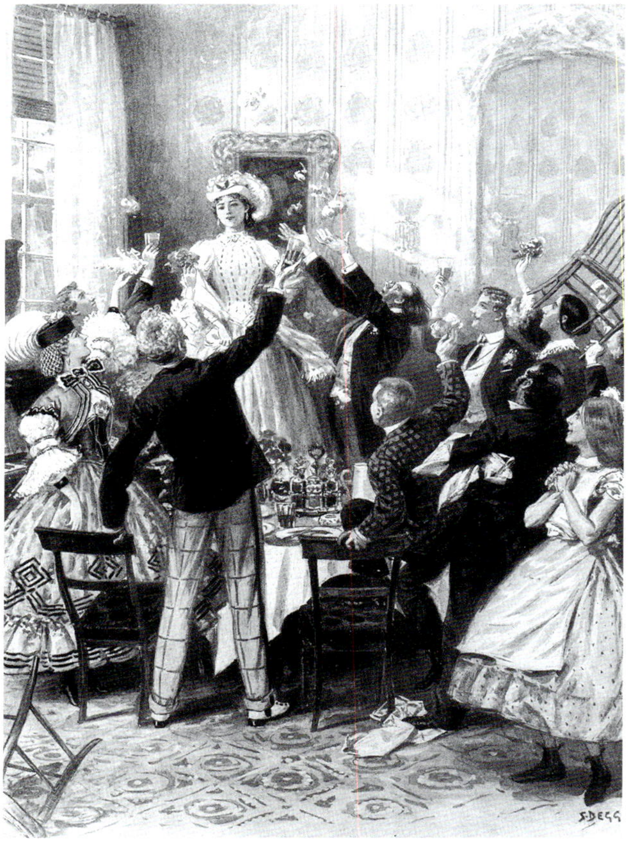

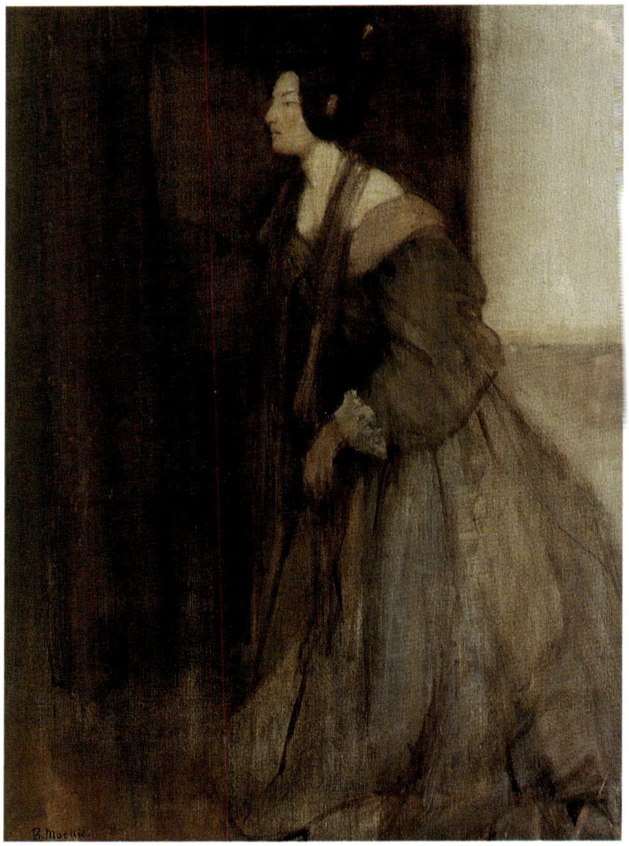

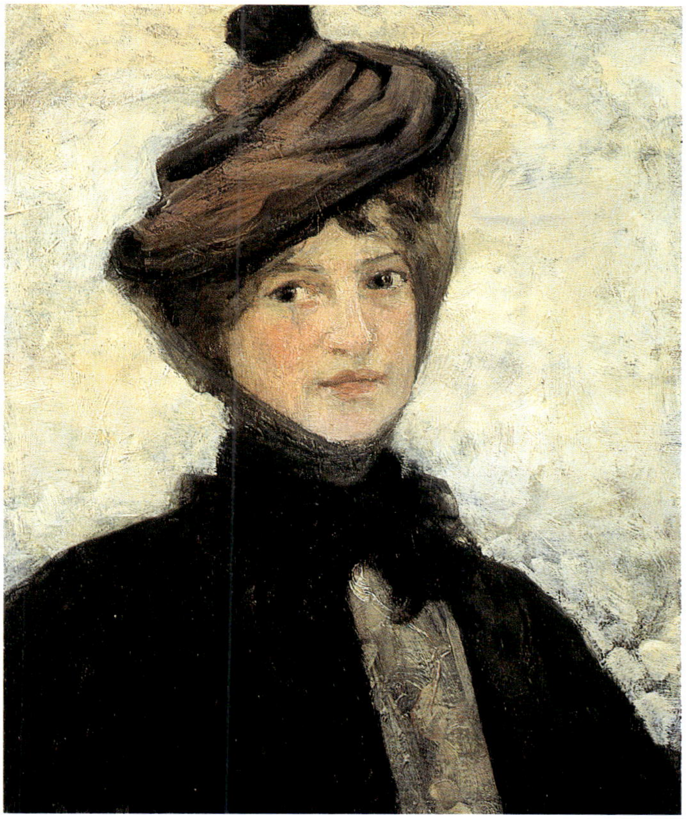

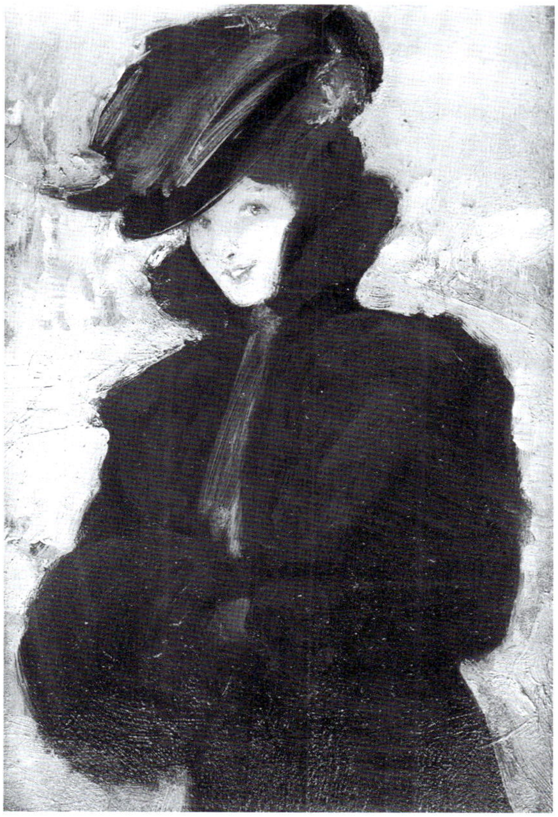

(above left)
PLATE 36
The Pink Hat
Oil on canvas
20x16
Private collection
(photo:R.M.Muirhead)

(above right)
PLATE 37
A Fashionable Young Lady
Oil on panel
11½x7¼
Private collection
(photo:Bourne Fine Art)

the extravagant accessories like ermine muffs and fans, parasols and hats with feather plumes. It is interesting to find that Kate Cranston, the famous restaurateur, shared her enthusiasm and wore a crinoline even in Edwardian Glasgow.

Did Bessie MacNicol perhaps see the January 1898 issue of *The Illustrated London News*, in which there is a full page illustration by S. Begg of Miss Rose Trelawny of the 'Wells' bidding goodbye to her theatrical friends on the eve of her marriage to Mr Gower?[3] (pl.34) On the left is Miss Imogen Parrott, dressed in a crinoline and a plumed pork pie hat and beaded chignon. This may have been the initial spark that set Bessie MacNicol to paint *A Girl of the 'Sixties'* (pl.43) exhibited for the first time in 1900. It is possible that she was in London in April 1898 and could have visited the New English Art Club Exhibition, at which Walter Richard Sickert showed his painting of Miss Hilda Spong as Imogen Parrot. Another painting by Bessie MacNicol *The Lace Cuff* (pl.35) may have been influenced by the costumes of *Trelawny of the Wells*. The young girl in her painting is more soberly dressed in black, but her hair style is similar to that of some of the characters in the play.

In the same issue of *The Illustrated London News* is a modest advertisement for Poncelet's Pastilles, in which a young girl is seen in wintry weather wearing a romantic hat with black feathers. This advertisement was by

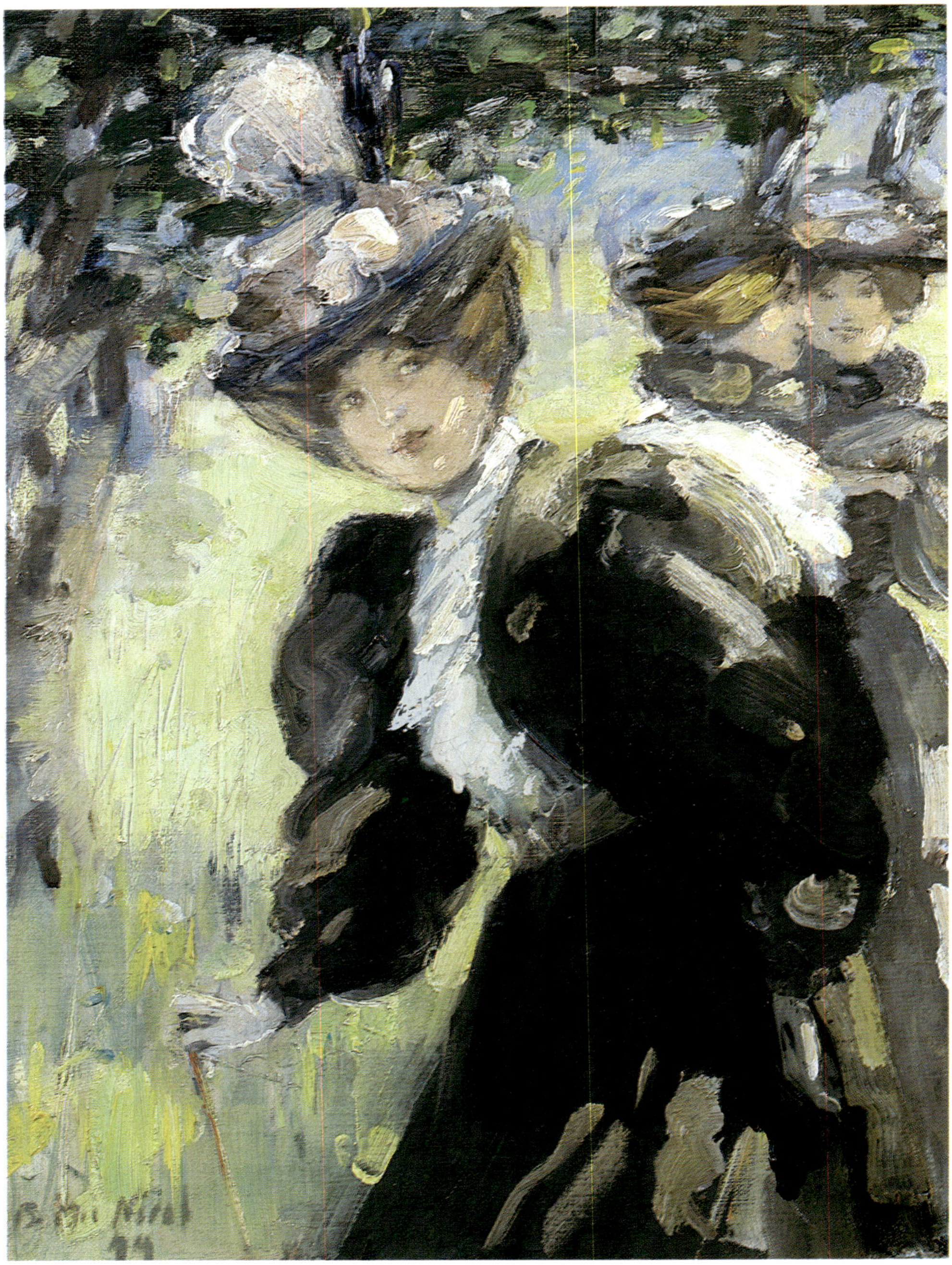

PLATE 38
In the Park
Oil on canvas
16x12
Private collection
(photo:Richard Green)

Maurice Greiffenhagen, who in 1906 was to come north to be Professor of the School of Drawing and Painting at Glasgow School of Art. It is reminiscent of a small undated painting by Bessie MacNicol now titled *A Fashionable Young Lady* (pl.37), but its original title could have been *Winter*. It is one of a group of very attractive small oil paintings painted at this time, which also includes *In the Park* (pl.38).

Bessie MacNicol's interest was not exclusively in dress of the past. She was also receptive to current fashions. This was a very romantic period in dress with a special interest in extravagant hats, as can be seen in *A Fashionable Young Lady*. In another attractive painting *The Pink Hat* (pl.36) the young woman is wearing a turban or glorified tammy with a pompon on top rather than a hat. The sitter is not known, but in 1898 – the date of the painting – the only portrait of a woman exhibited by Bessie MacNicol was at Liverpool, when she showed a work titled *A Daughter of Firenze*.

In these smaller paintings the women are wearing contemporary dress. Though they are slighter works in comparison with her more considerable ones, they are full of charm, vitality and movement. They are the equivalents in painting of Sir Thomas Beecham's attractive concert 'lollipops' or, to use one of her own words, little 'gems'.

1 *The Scots Pictorial* 28 May 1898 p.15
2 De Courcy L. Dewar, *History of the Glasgow Society of Lady Artists' Club* p.14
3 *The Illustrated London News* 29 January 1898 p.147

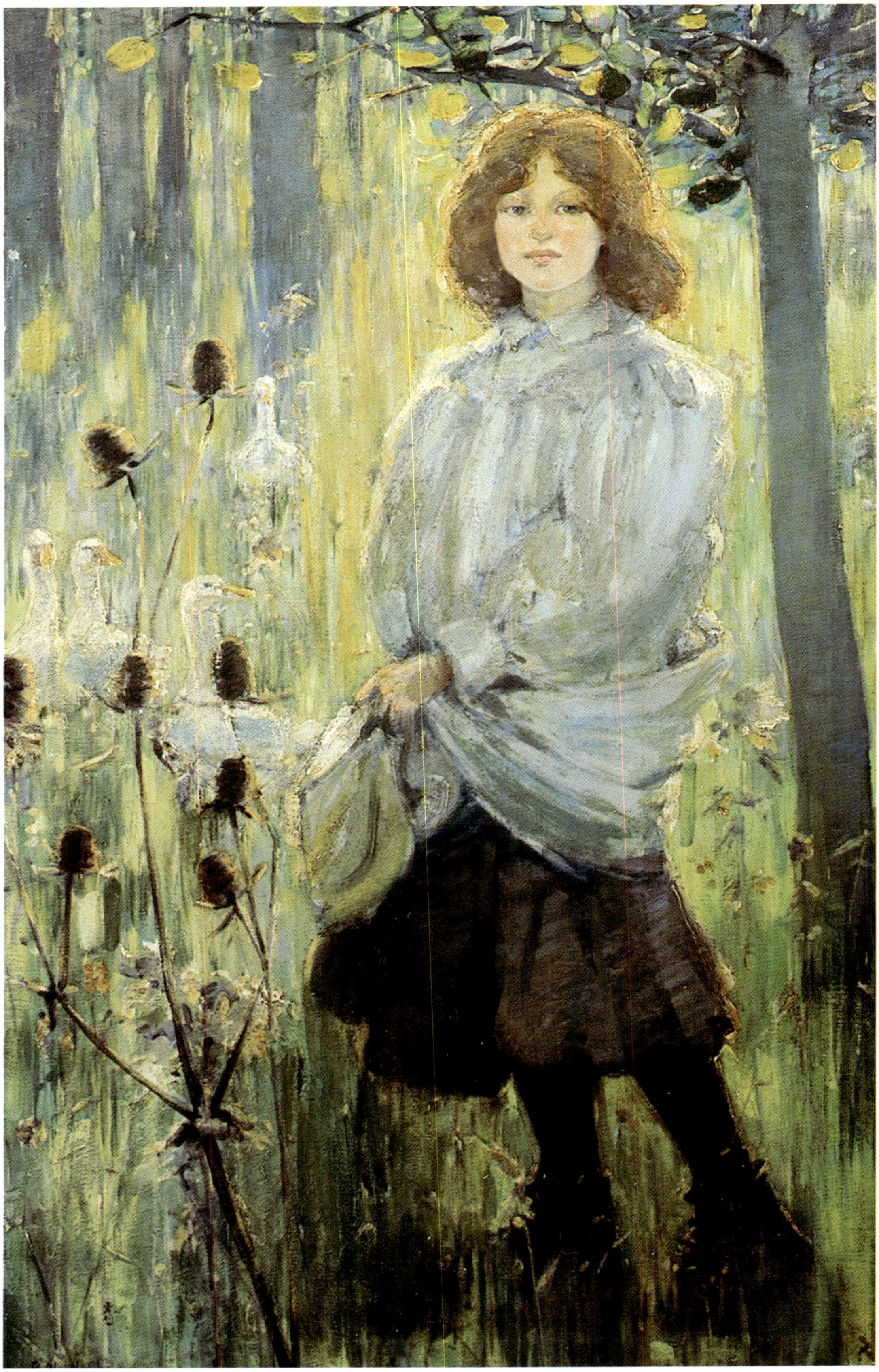

10. 1899

The Goose Girl (pl.39), the only work she exhibited at the Institute in 1899, is in complete contrast to her paintings of the 'sixties' or those of girls in contemporary fashions. This is a realist painting, in the style of Jules Bastien-Lepage, of a country girl wearing practical working boots, not fashionable shoes. The use of a tree at one side of the picture and the teazle plant in the left foreground are reminders of the painting by Bastien-Lepage in Glasgow Art Gallery of a little waif with sacking about her titled *Pauvre Fauvette* (pl.42). Could Bessie MacNicol have seen this painting or a reproduction in *The Art Journal* of 1896?[1] The little waif is referred to as the 'little cattle guardian' and the writer goes on to say 'This individual picture is probably better known in Britain than any other Bastien-Lepage painted.' At that time the picture belonged to George McCulloch, who may have lent it to exhibitions. It was lent in 1911 to the Glasgow Institute exhibition by Mrs. Coutts Michie and was purchased by Glasgow Art Gallery in 1913.

The young Glasgow Boys were greatly influenced by Bastien-Lepage's paintings of ordinary country people in the village of Damvilliers. James Guthrie painted *To Pastures New*, a small girl herding a gaggle of geese, a subject he had first seen at Crowland in Lincolnshire in the winter of 1883, although it had been tackled earlier by David Murray. There is an article in *The Scottish Art Review*, the magazine started by the Glasgow Boys in 1889, titled 'Bastien-Lepage and Realism' by George Clausen, whose works owe a great deal to Bastien-Lepage.[2] Clausen's *The Stone Pickers*, now in the Laing Art Gallery, Newcastle-upon-Tyne, is in the same realist tradition followed by Glasgow painters Guthrie, Crawhall, Henry and Walton while working with Guthrie at Cockburnspath in the 1880s.

The studies for *The Goose Girl* were made at Lundin Links when Bessie MacNicol was still a student, but obviously a great deal of work was done afterwards to prepare it for exhibition. The girl is seen against the sunlight, which appears as an aura around her. The design of the painting is very effective and the only weakness is the hand holding up her smock. Hands always gave Bessie MacNicol problems. Very often she dodged the issue by hiding them behind a bunch of flowers or by putting them into a muff. *The Goose Girl* brought favourable reviews from critics. The *Glasgow Herald* remarked that it was '. . . spiritually imagined and ably painted.'[3] It was sent to London in 1900 to the Women's International Exhibition at Earl's Court and was illustrated in a review of the exhibition in *The Studio*.[4] It is interesting to compare the painting with the reproduction. It can be seen that some alteration has been made to the girl's features and hair. It was quite customary for Bessie MacNicol to alter paintings on their return from exhibitions.

(opposite)
PLATE 39
The Goose Girl
Oil on canvas
51½x32
Private collection
(photo:A.G.Ingram)

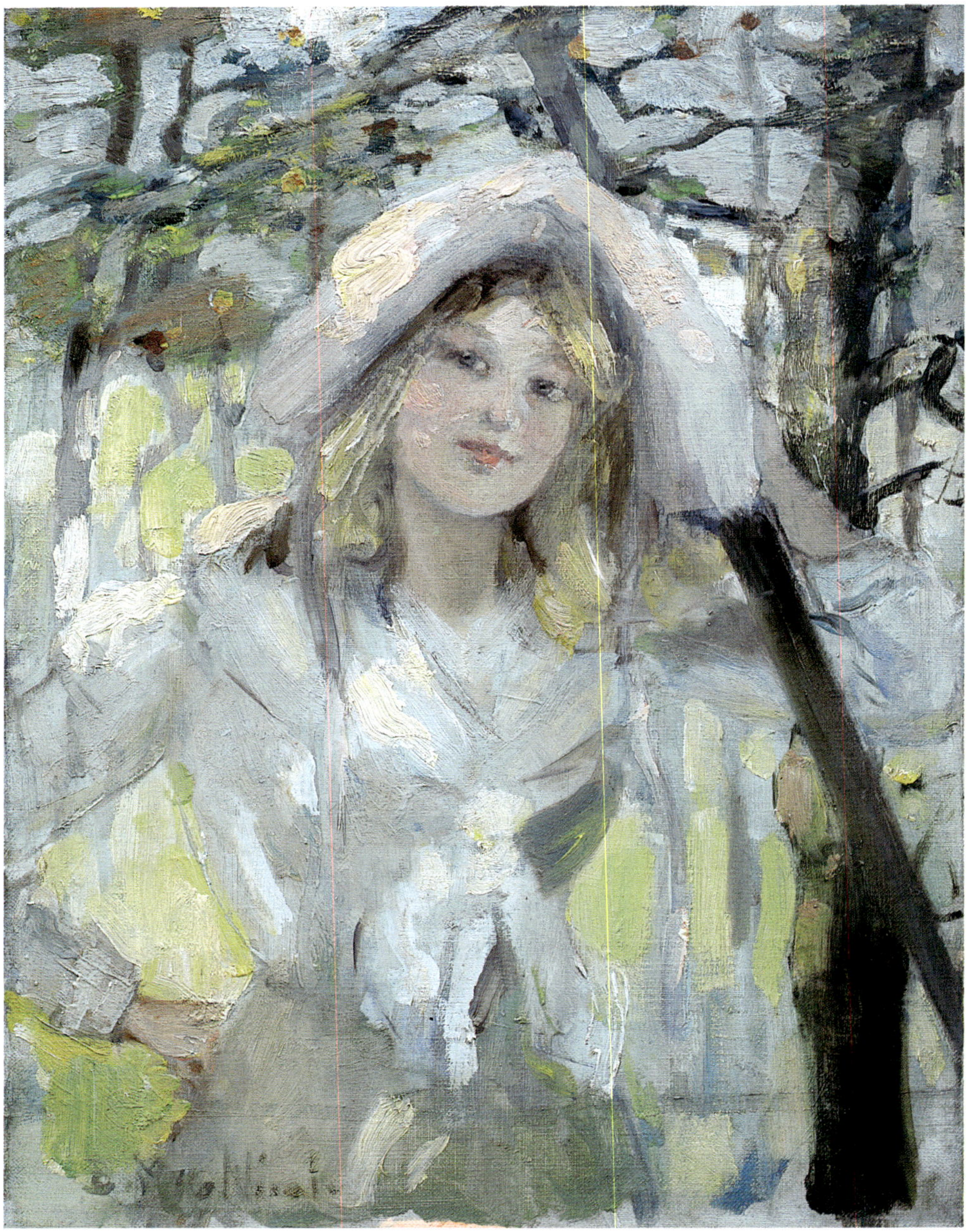

PLATE 40
The Lilac Sunbonnet
Oil on canvas
16x12
Mrs Rita Skelly
(photo:Richard Green)

Also executed at this time were more decorative works of women field-workers wearing large cotton sunbonnets. The girl in *The Lilac Sunbonnet* (pl.40) is leaning on the handle of a hay-fork. This is one of two versions of the same subject. *Girl in Sunbonnet* (pl.41) in Perth Art Gallery shows the head and shoulders of a young girl wearing a field-worker's protective headgear.

Exhibition at Stephen T. Gooden's Art Rooms

Earlier Bessie MacNicol held her one and only solo exhibition at Stephen T. Gooden's Art Rooms, 62 Renfield Street from 17th to 27th January 1899.

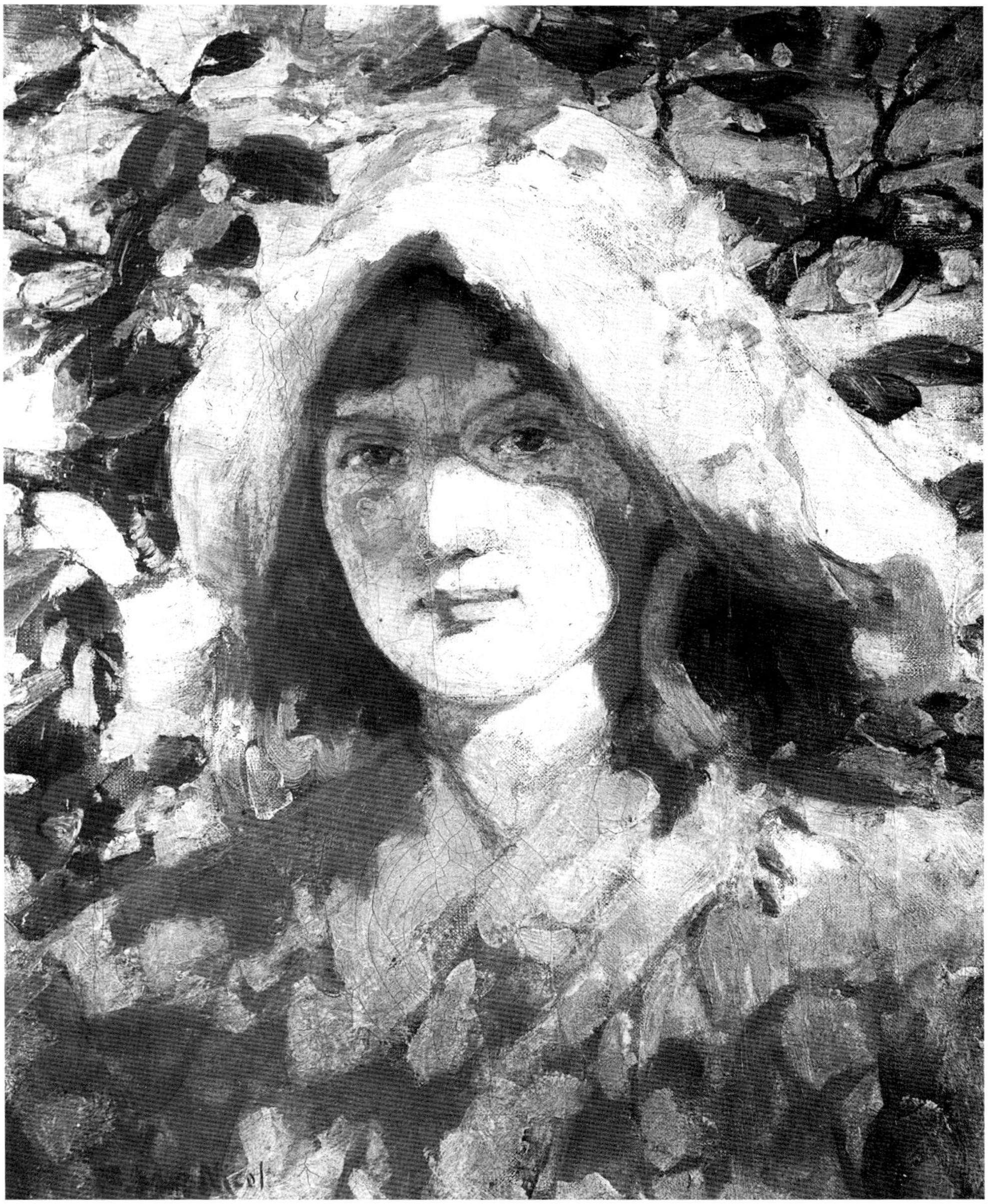

PLATE 41
Girl in Sunbonnet
Oil on canvas
19½x15½
Perth Museum & Art Gallery, Perth & Kinross Council

This important event in her life appears to have passed without much notice, but it was held at a bad time of year. During the exhibition the weather was particularly inclement with gales and snow. The only important notice was in the *Glasgow Herald*. The critic noted the influence of Whistler in *Twilight* and *The Lady in Green* (both untraced) and continued:

> . . . and in other pictures we find evidence of sympathy with less distinguished artists. But these are mere suggestions, which more than anything will attest the width of her range of feeling and accomplishment, Miss M'Nicol's exhibition, as we have indicated, is one of distinct achievement.[5]

Compared with previous reviews this was praise indeed. Included in the exhibition was a portrait of Alexander Frew, to whom she was probably

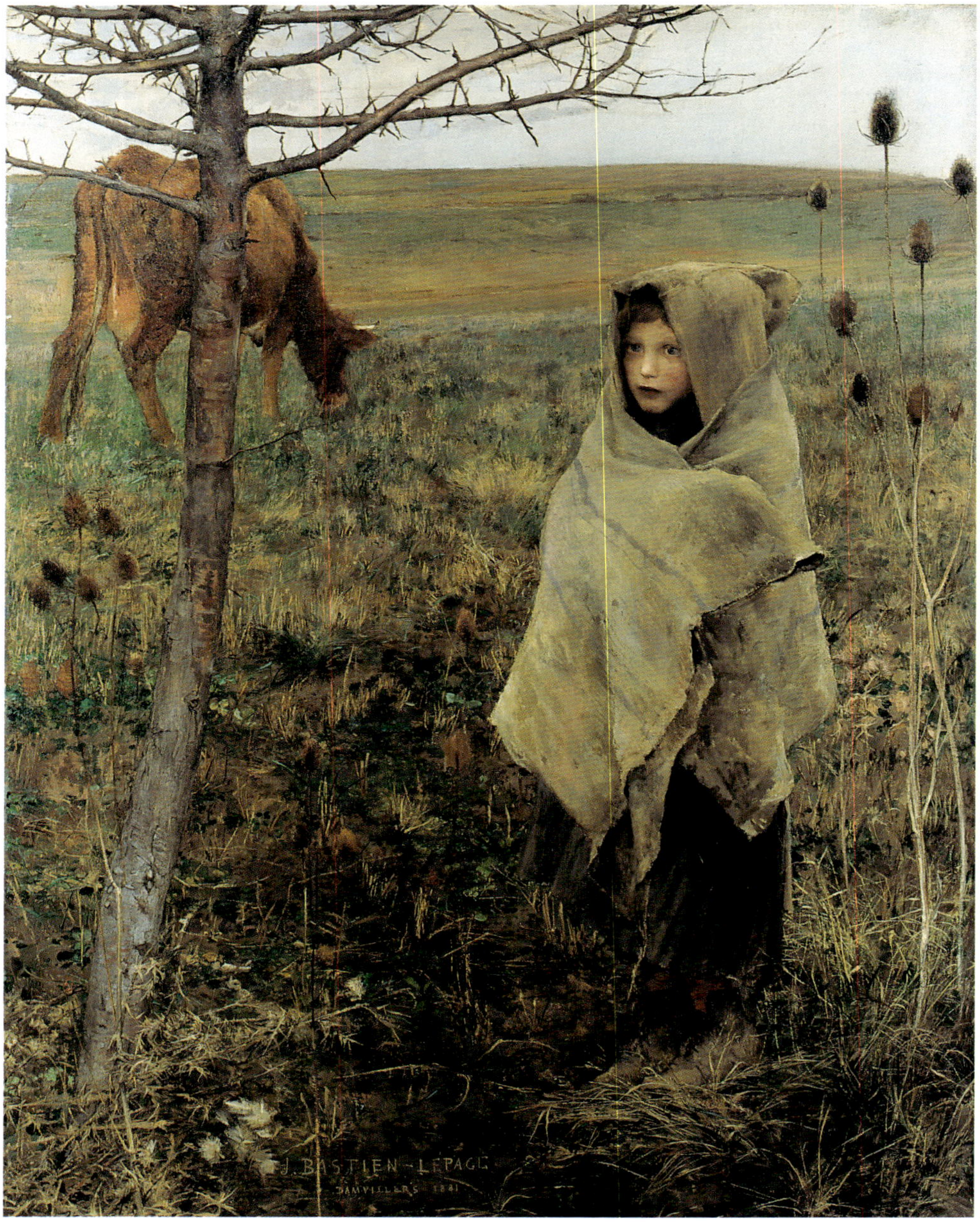

PLATE 42
JULES BASTIEN-LEPAGE
Pauvre Fauvette
Oil on canvas
64x49½
Glasgow Museums: Art Gallery & Museum, Kelvingrove

already engaged, because the marriage took place at her home at 4 Oakfield Terrace on 19th April 1899. The minister was an old friend of the bridegroom; Revd William Jeffrey, then minister of Kilsyth Free Church, had studied medicine before turning to the Church.

DR ALEXANDER FREW

Alexander Frew was a striking looking man with strong features and dark hair. He was also an outstandingly versatile man with many and varied interests. He had trained initially as a doctor at Glasgow University, graduating in 1884, and had also studied abroad at Leipzig and Vienna. He later specialised in obstetrics and gynaecology, obtaining his practical experience at the Rotunda Hospital in Dublin. After a start in practice in Glasgow he gave up medicine for art and became a full-time painter with a studio in St. Vincent Place. He painted mainly marine subjects, which were noted for their fine skies. He was well known to the Glasgow artists, being a member of Glasgow Art Club until he resigned in 1897. He can be considered a fringe member of the Glasgow Boys. His paintings of the sea were probably influenced by his love of yachting, for on his yacht *Ronaval* he sailed intrepidly round the West Coast of Scotland. On one occasion when his younger brother became very ill, it was difficult to contact him as he was somewhere out in the Hebrides.

Frew had many scientific interests. His first love was botany. A herbarium formed in his early years of study was considered a model of its kind. Later interests were shells and molluscs; his collection of molluscs was presented to the Hunterian Museum in the University of Glasgow. When he married Bessie MacNicol in 1899, he gave up his career as a full-time painter. After further study in Paris and Berlin, he resumed medical practice in Glasgow from 12 St. James Terrace, becoming well-known as a consultant in gynaecology. However he did not give up painting altogether, for he continued to exhibit at the Glasgow Institute until 1905.

The couple set up house in Hillhead at 12 St. James Terrace, now Ruskin Terrace, Great Western Road. The house had belonged to David Young Cameron, the well-known painter and etcher, who had lived there following his marriage to Jeanie Ure Maclaurin in 1896. However the Camerons did not stay there long, moving south to London in 1898, and the house was sold to Alexander Frew. Cameron had built a large studio in the garden at the rear of the house with Art Nouveau details possibly inspired by Charles Rennie Mackintosh, but more probably designed by Cameron himself. There is a metal balustraded gallery above the studio, which had good north facing top lighting. Here Bessie MacNicol was able to paint larger paintings.

It must have been at this time that the painting *Iona Cathedral - Moonlight* (untraced) was painted by her. It seems likely that Alexander Frew would wish to share his love of the Western Isles with his wife on their honeymoon. Frew himself exhibited *Iona Sands* at the Glasgow Institute in 1900.

1 *The Art Journal* 1896 p.201
2 *The Scottish Art Review* vol.I 1889 p.114
3 *Glasgow Herald* 4 February 1899
4 *The Studio* vol.XX 1900 p.182
5 *Glasgow Herald* 24 January 1899

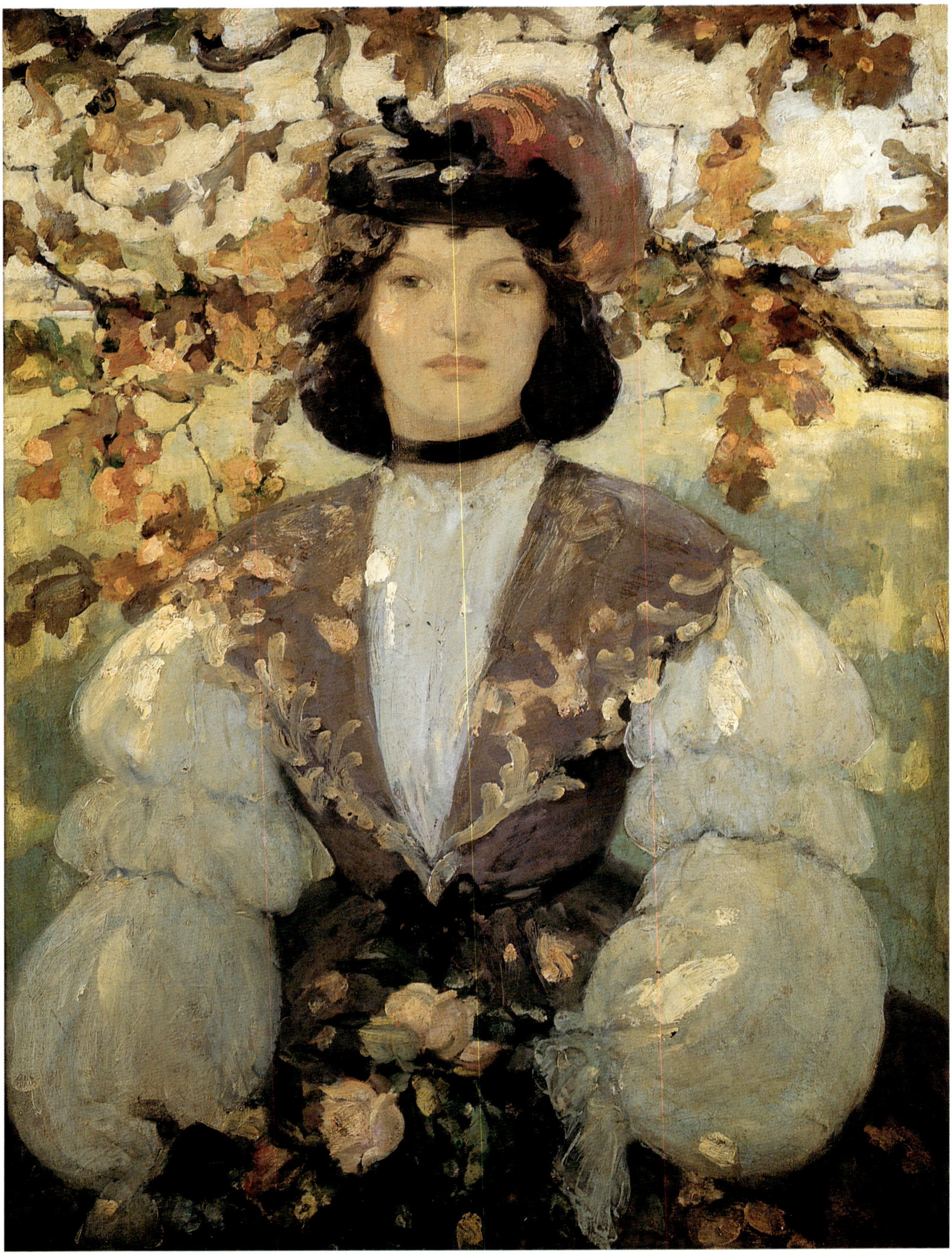

11. 1900

Bessie MacNicol's portrait of Alexander Frew (pl.44), which had been exhibited the previous January at Stephen T. Gooden's gallery, was sent to the Institute exhibition in 1900. Unfortunately this painting cannot now be traced. It was not listed in McTear's auction sale catalogue after Frew's death and present members of both families have no knowledge of it. As far as we know, it is the first portrait of a man she painted since her portrait of Hornel. Though we can only judge the painting from a reproduction, it looks to be a very strong and directly painted work of a strikingly handsome man.[1]

A Girl of the 'Sixties'

As well as Frew's portrait Bessie MacNicol exhibited *A Girl of the 'Sixties'* (pl.43), probably her most important fancy portrait of a young woman *en plein air* under the branches and leaves of an oak tree. Quite apart from the title of the picture, the influence of *Trelawny of the Wells* can be seen in this crinoline dressed girl, who is wearing a pork pie or, to give it its correct name, 'Montego' hat over hair tucked into a chignon. Once more the sun is filtering through the leaves and shining in little patches on her dress. This is a most attractive work, satisfactory in design and subtle in colour and very well painted. Tonally it works well too, the dark hair and hat and black choker ribbon framing the girl's face.

It was given an honoured place in the Third International Society Exhibition in London in 1901, eliciting a critical notice from Oswald Sickert, the father of Walter Richard Sickert, in *The Studio*.[2] Praise is given as well as criticism:

> . . . The painter who approaches the dealer's landscape is advanced, he has reached a stage where he may stop, his landscape is final of its kind, there is no reason why he should go further. Miss MacNicol's is a good example of the painting that settles down at an early stage. One is surprised that the struggle with the unmanageable medium of oil paint should be given up at this, or indeed at any stage, but because the painter reveals no quiver of inability anywhere in her picture – why then has she chosen to stop? The sky, as everyone has experienced who has drawn the outline of a branch of a tree with the background instead of upon it, is apt to project in front of the leaves. Miss MacNicol's sky has not come out in spite of her efforts, she likes it so; she has pulled it out between the leaves in cakes. What matters, however, about it, is not that the sky precedes the leaves – that is a matter of taste – but that the way of pushing the sky in and out among the leaves makes for ugly quality. Subtlety is not possible with such painting, and without an effort to reach a greater subtlety it is not likely that the quality of paint will grow finer. Miss MacNicol is still a realist, and if she remains one, it seems hardly necessary that just the fear of confessing anywhere to a little weakness, or lack of capacity, should keep her technique where it now stands.

(opposite)
PLATE 43
A Girl of the 'Sixties'
Oil on canvas
32x24
Glasgow Museums: Art Gallery & Museum, Kelvingrove

Hornel's work also received criticism from Oswald Sickert in the succeeding passage:

> It is different with Mr. Hornel. He has thrown over realistic pre-occupations, and raised the patchwork painting to the pitch of an art by itself . . . One argues that, after all a patchwork quilt, such as one used to find on country beds was often quite a pretty and an amusing thing, and Mr. Hornel has kindly added to the prettiness and amusement by cleverly fitting figures into his pieces, figures of children that may be made out quite easily.

One is left with the feeling that Bessie MacNicol has come off more lightly than Hornel, in that her promise has been noted and progress in technique hoped for, while Oswald Sickert has nothing to say to Hornel.

1 Percy Bate, op. cit. p.203
2 *The Studio* vol.XXIV 1902 pp.122-3

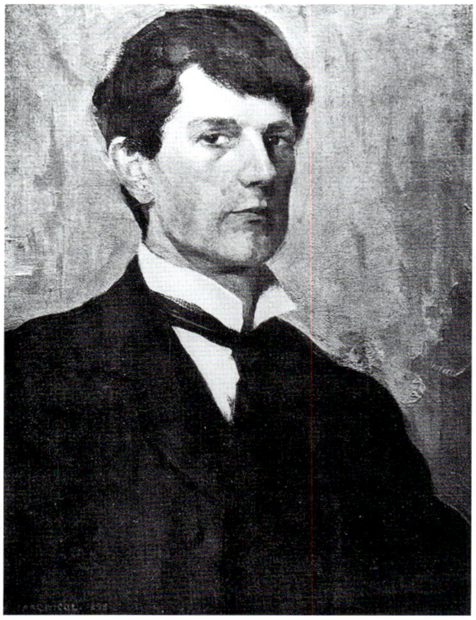

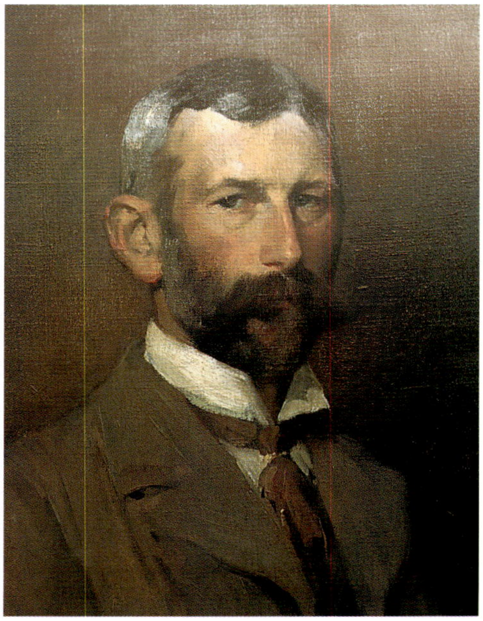

(left)
PLATE 44
Alexander Frew
Untraced
(photo:City of Glasgow Libraries & Archives, Mitchell Library)

(right)
PLATE 45
John Rennie (detail)
Oil on canvas
John Rennie
(photo:Marian Rennie Studio Gallery, Australia)

12. 1901

1901 was an important year of celebration for Glasgow. Preparations had been in progress for another exhibition since the close of the last International Exhibition in the city in 1888, which had made a profit of £41,700 according to the figure published in 1890. The summer-long International Exhibition in 1901 was also a great success and brought crowds of people to Kelvingrove. Focusing attention on the progressive industries and products that had made the City important, the Exhibition gave to Glaswegians a tremendous sense of civic pride.

Apart from the serious exhibits of engineering and manufactured goods, there was opportunity for all to enjoy the activities on the River Kelvin – the 'Water Chute' and the Venetian gondolas, which had been there in 1888 and were back again in 1901. Sculpture, painting and the decorative arts were well represented in the fine new building, which had been built with the profits of the earlier Exhibition and now played an important part in the 1901 Exhibition. Indeed the main entrance to this building – the present Kelvingrove Art Galleries – still faces the Park, as it did in 1901, with the elaborate statuary of St. Mungo by George Frampton on the entrance staircase.

In the exhibition catalogue of paintings by contemporary artists there is just one painting by Bessie MacNicol. *Apple Blossom* (431) was lent by the artist. This painting is possibly still in the possession of the artist's family. It was exhibited in her Memorial Exhibition in 1905 and was in Robert McTear's Auction Sale after Alexander Frew's death in 1908. This must have been the first of her *en plein air* portraits of girls under leafy branches.

Portraits of Men

At the Spring Exhibition of the Glasgow Institute in 1901 Bessie MacNicol showed two further portraits of men. Though both paintings are entered in the catalogue as simply 'Portrait', one (pl.45) can be identified as John Rennie, an accountant who lived in Helensburgh and was a friend of Alexander Frew. The other portrait was probably of William Lamont, another Helensburgh friend, who was an accountant and stockbroker. He became acting secretary to the Glasgow Society of Artists when it was formed the following year.

Portraits of the Artist's Sisters

Having in mind the crowds of visitors that would come to Glasgow in the summer of 1901, the Institute decided to hold a further exhibition in addition to its Annual Exhibition. It opened in July at the Fine Art Institute in Sauchiehall Street. Unfortunately the crowds went to Kelvingrove and did

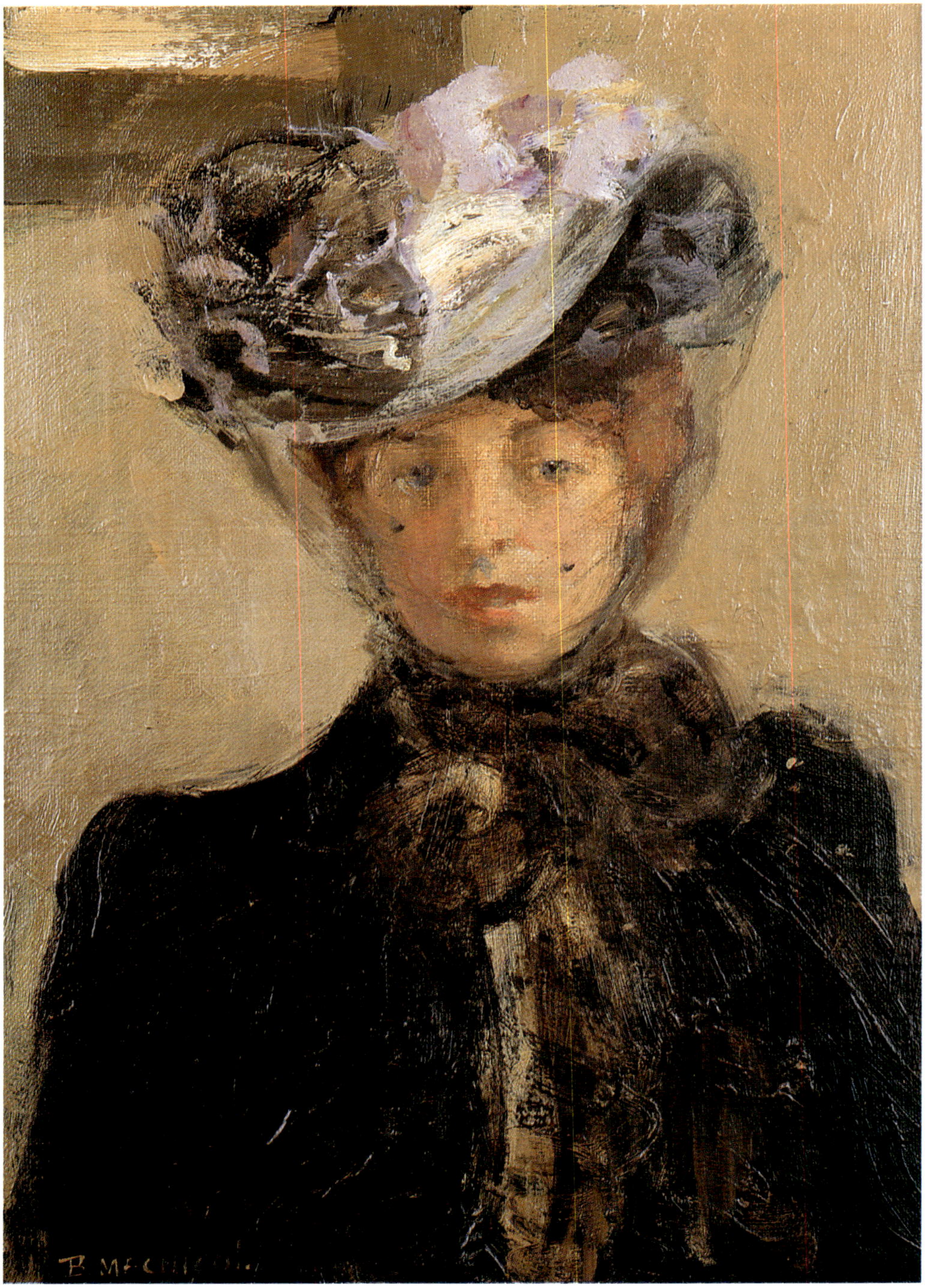

PLATE 46
The Veiled Hat
Oil on canvas
$11x8\frac{3}{4}$
Private collection
(photo:A.Gorzkowski)

not come into the centre of the city. Consequently the exhibition was not a financial success. Bessie MacNicol showed *Tritomas* and three other works, two of which were probably watercolours or small works modestly priced. The fourth was *Portrait of the Artist's Sister* (pl.47), which was not for sale. This may have been of her sister Janet – or Jessie as she was called – and is dated 1900. Jessie had been a music student at the Glasgow Athenaeum

PLATE 47
Portrait of the Artist's Sister
Oil on canvas
32x26
Private collection
(photo:R.M.Muirhead)

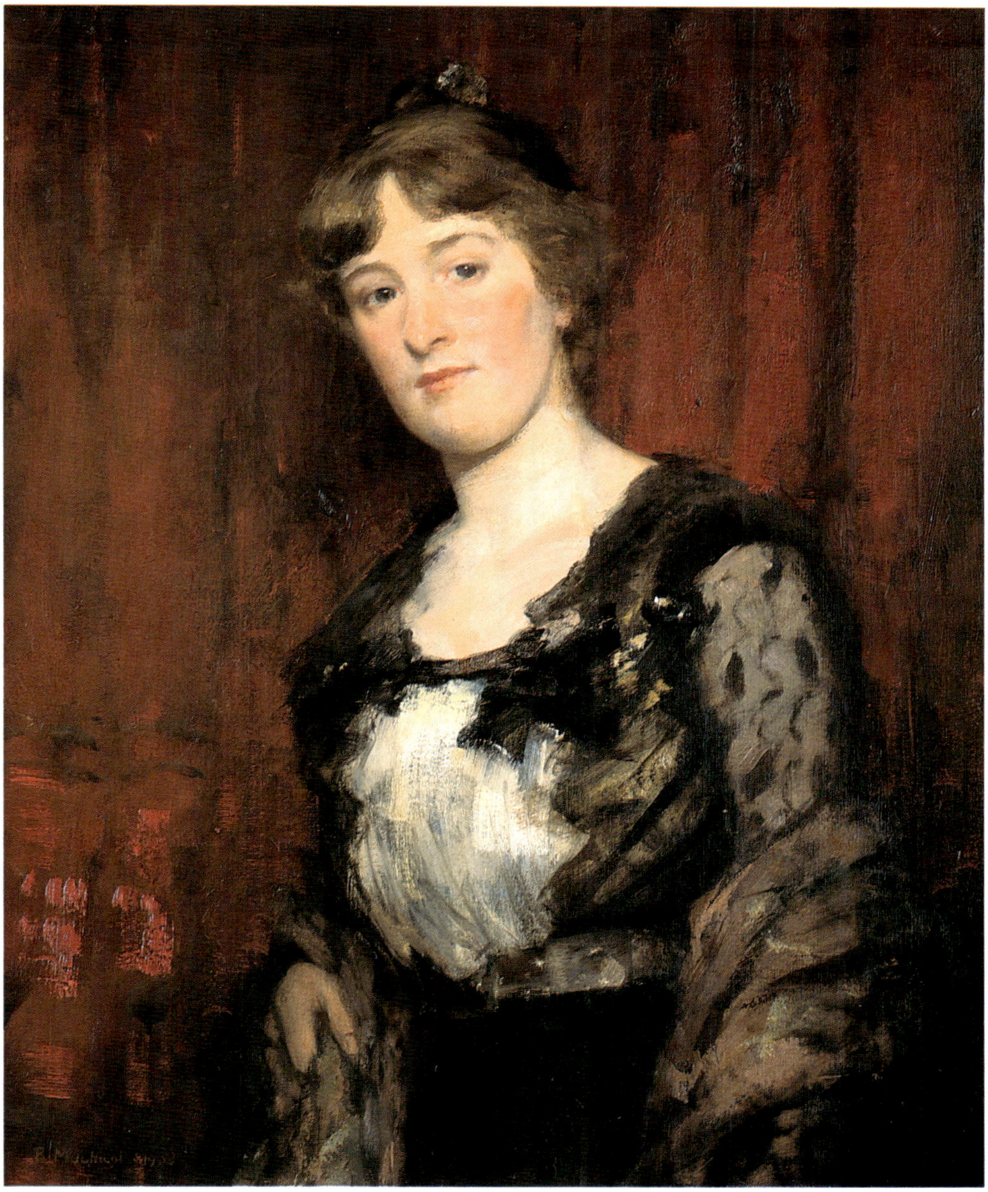

from 1892 until 1894, but there is no record of what she did afterwards. She is not listed as a teacher of music in the Glasgow directory, but she may have taught in a private school or taken piano students privately. On 30th January 1903 she married Daniel Frew (not a near relation of Alexander Frew). He was an analytical chemist, who had been on the staff of Glasgow School of Art as lecturer on chemistry of colours in 1902. They went to live in Sydenham in Kent. There is no further information on her until her death at the age of 62 on 5th June 1933 at Longmore Hospital in Edinburgh. Then she was a widow living at Bonnyrigg near Edinburgh. It is a very sympathetic portrait of her sister, who one senses was of a quieter disposition and had a shyer nature than Bessie MacNicol herself.

Minnie Phoebe MacNicol

Bessie MacNicol's younger sister Minnie Phoebe was married to Victor Lionel Alexander on 2nd April 1901. Minnie, like her sister Jessie, had been a music student at the Glasgow Athenaeum. Possibly she had met her husband there. Alexander was interested in the theatre and had appeared in several productions at the Athenaeum Theatre. His grandfather John Henry Alexander (1796-1851) had been an actor-manager and one of the personalities of his day in Glasgow. In 1840 he made extensive alterations to the Caledonian Theatre in Dunlop Street and changed its name to Theatre Royal, the earlier theatre of that name having been destroyed by fire.

Bessie MacNicol was particularly fond of painting her younger sister in oils, watercolour and pastel. At the time of her marriage she painted portraits of both the newly-weds. Minnie is wearing her going-away clothes, a red brown suit trimmed with fur and a fur muff. A pastel has been retained by the Alexander family, portraying the newly-wed Mrs Alexander putting on her gloves before going on honeymoon. Minnie had a very attractive face and very characteristic, slightly protruding teeth, which betray her identity unmistakably.

This can be seen in the most attractive small oil painting of Minnie, *The Veiled Hat* (pl.46), which is not dated. It is one of the loveliest pictures Bessie MacNicol ever painted. Though small in scale, it is a most sensitive study and may have been painted shortly before her sister's marriage. An earlier, particularly fine watercolour, very directly painted, which is still in the artist's family, shows her dressed perhaps for the Fancy Dress Ball of 1896 with a large bonnet and carrying a cloth pocket like the nursery rhyme character 'Lucy Locket'.

Lamplight

Minnie may have been the model for the painting titled *Lamplight*, which according to Percy Bate was 'one of the first of her portrait studies.'[1] Indeed there may be two paintings with this title. A painting titled *Lamplight* was exhibited in the St. Louis Exposition of 1896 (329) and was possibly shown again at Venice in 1899 (31). A possible second painting also titled *Lamplight* was executed in 1901 or perhaps the first work was altered and then redated. This work must have been painted at night using artificial light, as a large dark shadow is cast by the figure – especially by the head – on the wall behind. Another picture which was obviously painted in electric light, and in which a strong shadow is cast behind the sitter, is *Jonquils* (pl.51) by Philip Wilson Steer, which was exhibited at the New English Art Club in 1890. It was illustrated in *The Art Journal* for that year and one wonders whether Bessie MacNicol might have seen it.[2] *Lamplight* (pl.48) is a very stylish portrait of a young girl in black evening dress with a black choker ribbon round her neck. Spread out at her waist

(opposite)
PLATE 48
Lamplight
Oil on canvas
30x25
Hunterian Art Gallery, University of Glasgow

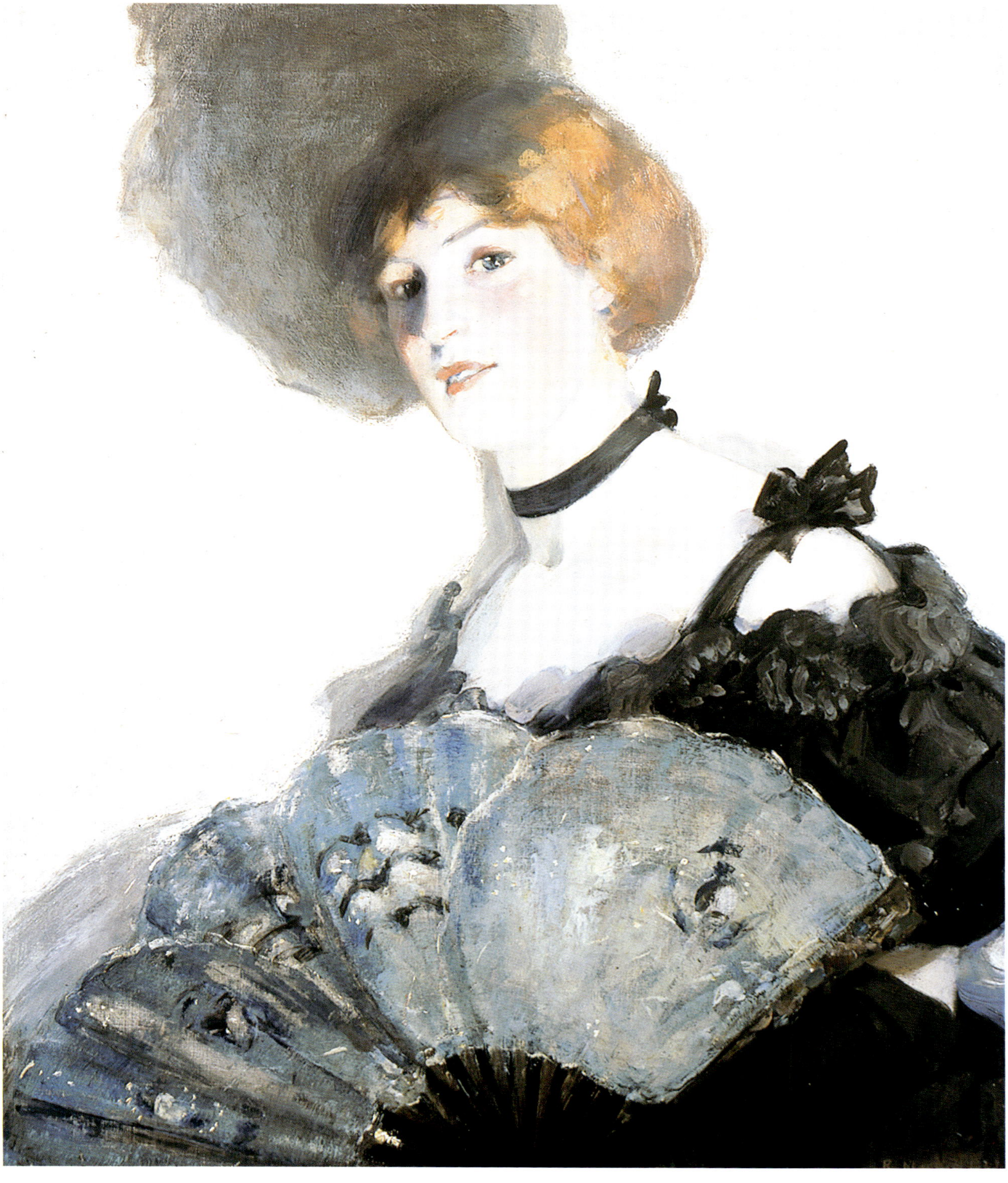

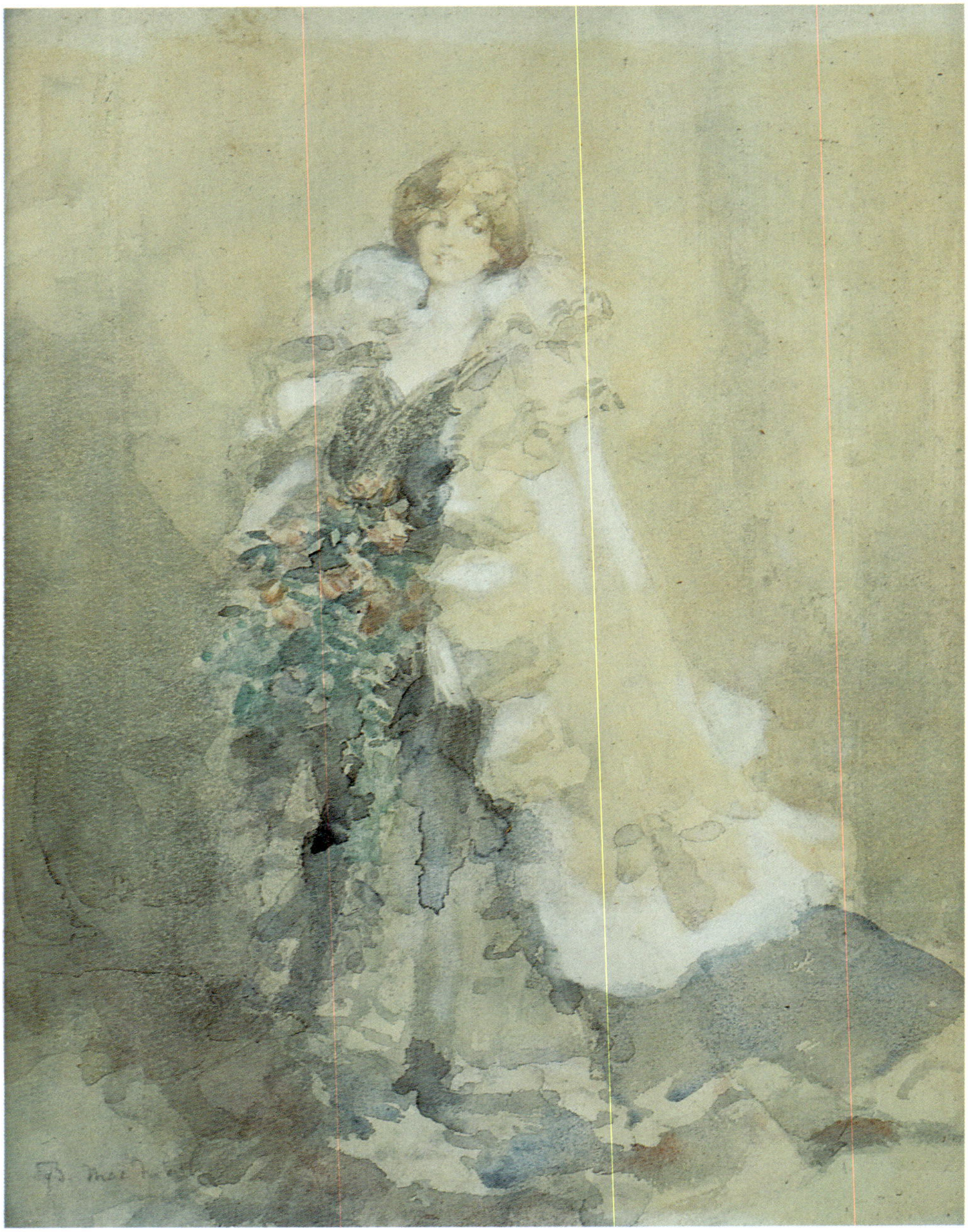

PLATE 49
Princess Charming
Watercolour
9½x7½
Private collection
(photo:R.M.Muirhead)

is a spangled silk fan. This painting was presented to the Hunterian Art Gallery by the late Prof. Alec Macfie in 1977.

WATERCOLOURS

Around this period Bessie MacNicol painted watercolours, usually of women wearing the crinoline dresses of the sixties. These watercolours are very sensitively and delicately executed. They show an appreciation of the breadth possible in this medium and demonstrate a respect for the 'wetness' of its character. Unfortunately several have faded by being hung in too strong a light. One of the most beautiful must be *Princess Charming* (pl.49), a girl wearing cascades of frills round the edges of her wrap. The watercolour medium presents another facet of Bessie MacNicol's work. I think it was her sensitive appreciation of the possibilities of this medium and her ability to realise more intimate subjects on a smaller scale that makes her watercolours so different from her oil paintings, yet very special in their own way.

1 Percy Bate, op. cit. p.201
2 *The Art Journal* 1890 p.157

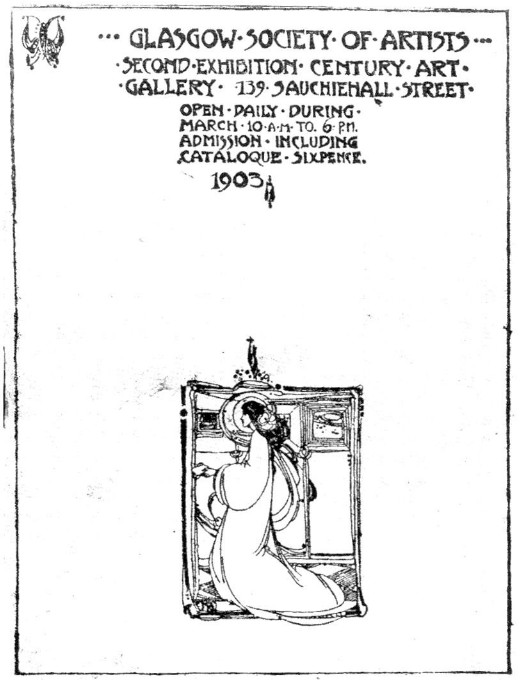

PLATE 50
JESSIE M. KING
Cover for Catalogue
National Library of Scotland
(© Dumfries & Galloway Council
& The National Trust for
Scotland)

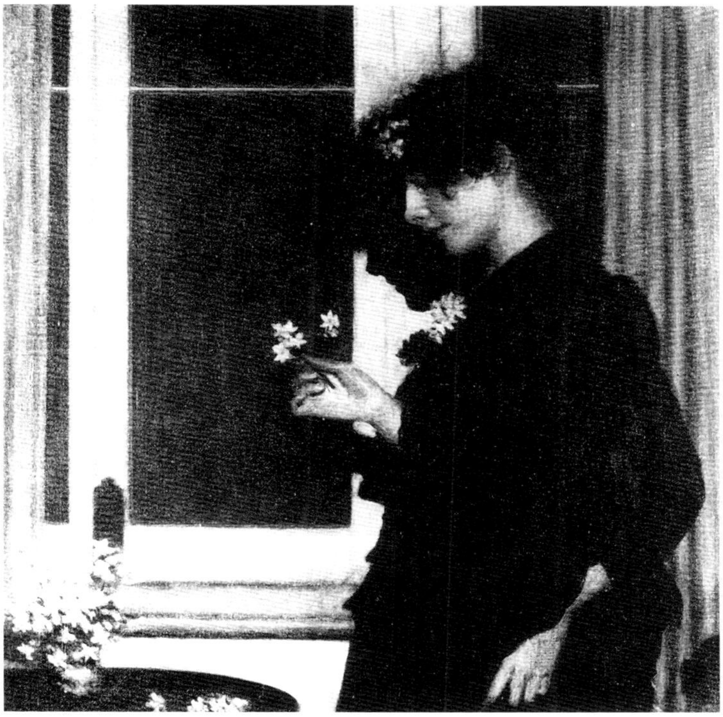

PLATE 51
PHILIP WILSON STEER
Jonquils
© Tate Gallery
(photo:City of Glasgow
Libraries & Archives,
Mitchell Library)

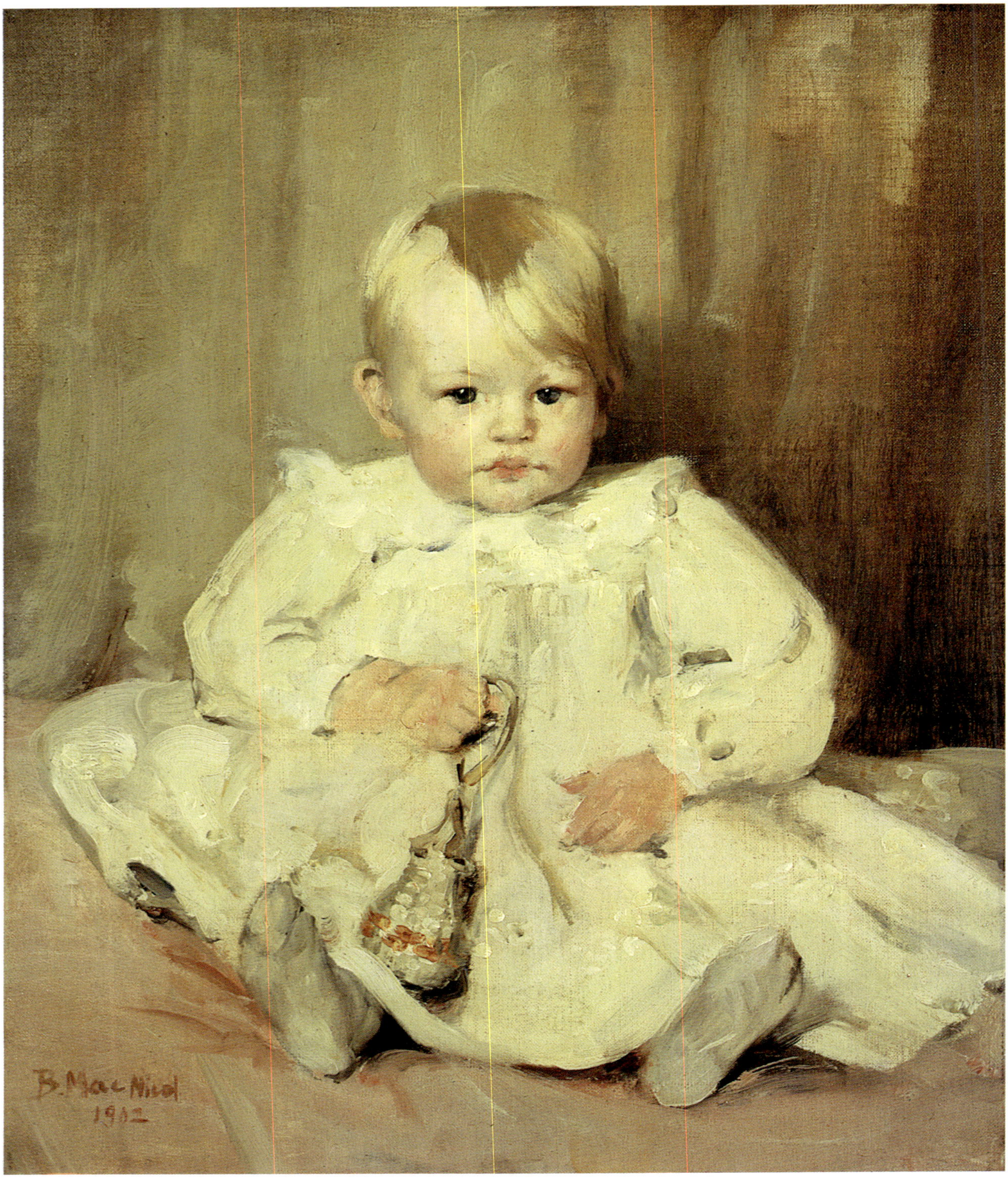
B. Mac Nicol
1912

13. 1902

Bessie MacNicol sent two paintings to the Glasgow Institute in 1902, *Mr. Edgar Barratt* and *Baby Crawford.* Albert Edgar Barratt was another Helensburgh friend, the organist and choirmaster at the West Parish Church in Helensburgh, whose minister at that time was the Revd John Baird, father of John Logie Baird, one of the pioneers in the invention of television. Barratt had studied music at Leipzig and Oxford and at one time played with the Scottish Orchestra. He also taught music as a visiting professor at St Bride's, a girl's school in Helensburgh. He may have been a yachting companion of Alexander Frew, because in his obituary in the *Glasgow Herald* it states that he was just back from a yachting holiday when he died at his home at 13 Kersland Street, Glasgow on 20th August 1928.[1] *Mr. Edgar Barratt* has not been traced, as is the case with so many other paintings by Bessie MacNicol.

Baby Crawford

The other painting exhibited at the Institute that year was *Baby Crawford* (pl.52), a delightful study of a baby. At first glance it is difficult to tell whether the infant is a girl or a boy, as babies wore identical clothes at that time. However this is a baby boy, who stares so unblinkingly and with such great interest at the painter and the viewer. He is John William Croom Crawford, born on 13th January 1901 the eldest son of Glasgow architect John Maclean Crawford, who in October 1897 had married Jenny Blackwood Brown, a Helensburgh friend of the artist. The Crawfords had two other children, James and Teresa. When the MacNicol home at 4 Oakfield Terrace had to be sold on the death of Peter MacNicol in 1903, it was bought by Jenny Crawford.

When this painting was shown at the Fourth Exhibition of the Glasgow Society of Artists at the Doré Gallery in London in 1905, the London critic of the *Glasgow Evening Times* wrote:

> It is the finest, and at the same time, the saddest part of the show to find the remarkable advance in her art from 1899 . . . to Baby painted in 1902, which I think is her masterpiece . . . It is of course, a picture that would attract attention anywhere, but, besides the tender subtle modelling of the baby, the delicate gentle colour, the eyes so babylike and startlingly blue in the indeterminate face, as well as the graceful unity of the whole, the later picture seems a different kind of thing. This is a picture which Glasgow Corporation would do well to purchase. It would hold its place with almost anything inside the Glasgow Galleries.[2]

(opposite)
PLATE 52
Baby Crawford
Oil on canvas
24¼x20
The City Art Centre, Edinburgh

Arthur Kay, the writer, art connoisseur and collector, bought *Baby Crawford* in 1908, most probably at the Royal Exchange Salerooms of Robert McTear, following the death of Alexander Frew, when it was listed as 'A Baby's

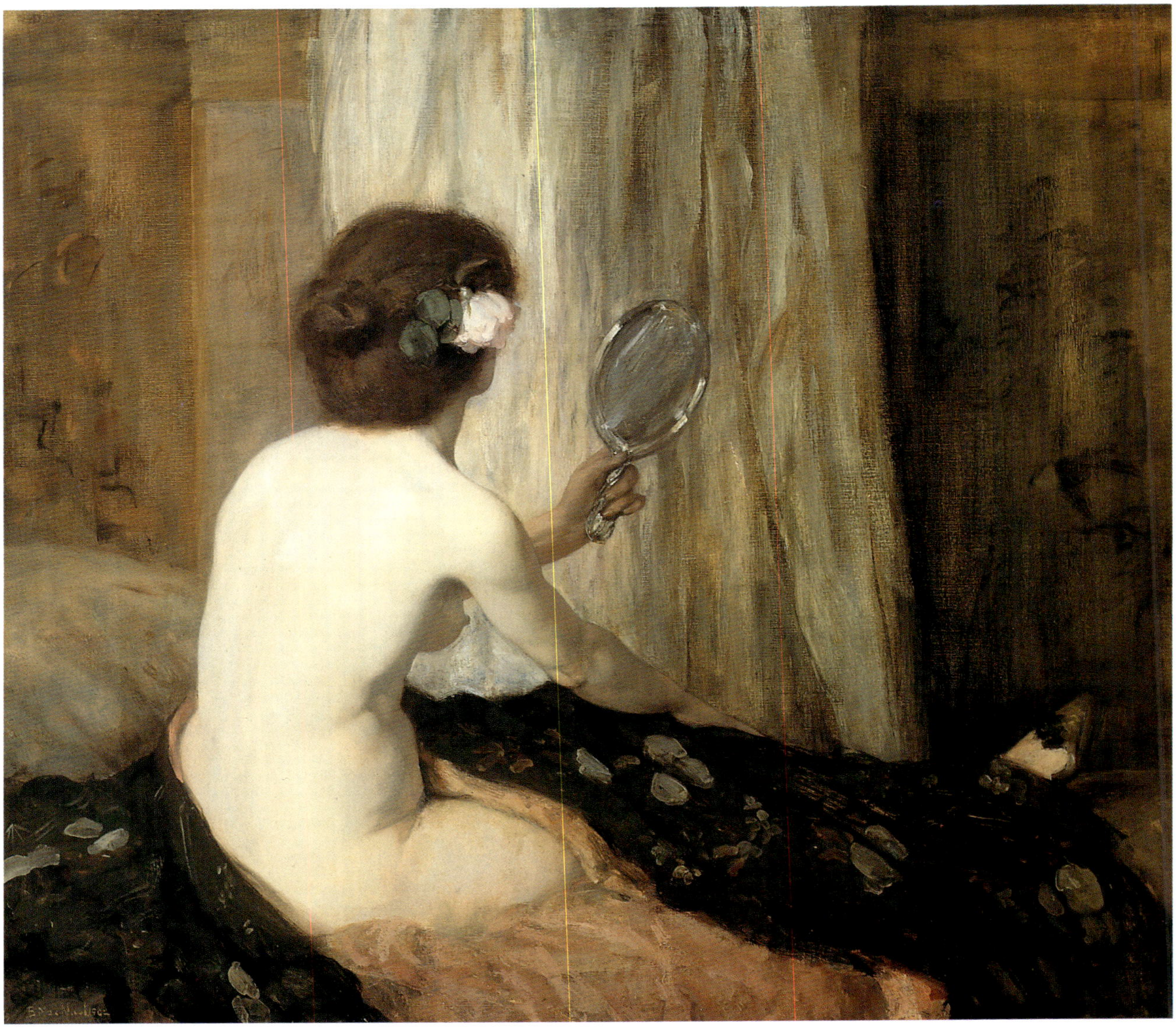

Portrait' (66). Kay presented it the same year to the Scottish Modern Arts Association. In 1964 most of the works owned by the Association were accepted by the City of Edinburgh Art Collection, including *Baby Crawford.*

PLATE 53
Vanity
Oil on canvas
45x50¼
Private collection
(photo:Sotheby's)

Glasgow Society of Artists' First Exhibition

For some time now there had been growing criticism of the Royal Glasgow Institute and the undue influence of laymen in its administration. This was voiced in the correspondence columns of the *Glasgow Herald* in February and March 1902. The prime mover for a new society to be formed for artists and under artists' control was Alexander Frew. The aims of the new Glasgow Society of Artists were to bring together Glasgow and West of Scotland artists and international artists, somewhat in the manner of the International Society in London. This was never realised, however, as the majority of the members of Glasgow Art Club did not wish to be associated with the Society. They chose to make their decision public in the Glasgow periodical *The Bailie*, in which the names of about fifty members are listed.[3]

Membership of the new Society was to be restricted to thirty, but at the First Exhibition held in April at Warneuke's Galleries at 153 Sauchiehall Street (while the Institute exhibition was still running) only twenty-one members exhibited. The critic of the *Glasgow Herald* commented:

> The exhibition, therefore, is not so much the varied offering of a broadly-constituted society as that of a numerically small brotherhood who make combined appeal to public favour. Considering the largeness of its aims, the Glasgow Society of Artists is illustrative of the unrest of young men in a hurry. To what heights it may yet attain we shall not venture to prophesy.[4]

The Bailie's art columnist *Megilp* wrote:

> . . . The exhibition of the Glasgow Society of Artists comes to an end next week. It has been called the three man or two man one woman exhibition as between them three members exhibit 47 works (out of 134).[5]

The three artists were Alexander Frew, William Alfred Gibson and Bessie MacNicol. She showed seventeen works; ten were oils and the remainder drawings and watercolours. The more important of those were *Vanity*, *Lamplight* and *The Leghorn Hat.*

Vanity

The centrepiece of the paintings shown by Bessie MacNicol was undoubtedly *Vanity* (pl.53). This was the largest picture she had painted and it is an astonishing *tour de force*. The nude back of a young woman is seen as she bends slightly forward to look at herself in a hand mirror. Her legs are covered with a dark embroidery, possibly Japanese, its colour echoed in her dark hair. This was a subject in the tradition of the old masters. It hints at a recent viewing of *The Toilet of Venus* by Velasquez. However that painting was not hanging in the National Gallery until 1906, when it was presented by the National Art Collections Fund after its purchase from H. E. Morritt of Rokeby Hall. Consequently it was probably a reproduction that triggered her interest, though the painting was on loan to the Royal Academy in 1890. *Vanity* is Bessie MacNicol's own interpretation of the subject. Unlike *The Toilet of Venus* the reflection of the girl's face cannot be seen in the mirror and the colour scheme, though rich, is more subdued in tone. Both paintings do admirably express the feel of soft drapery on bare flesh. In *Vanity* the feeling for form in the slightly bent back and the painting of flesh has been exquisitely realised. The tonal changes are extremely subtle and most sensitively noted. The drawing of the receding right arm is most convincing, but a critic did take exception to the lower part of the body. Indeed there is some evidence to indicate that repainting has been done in that area.

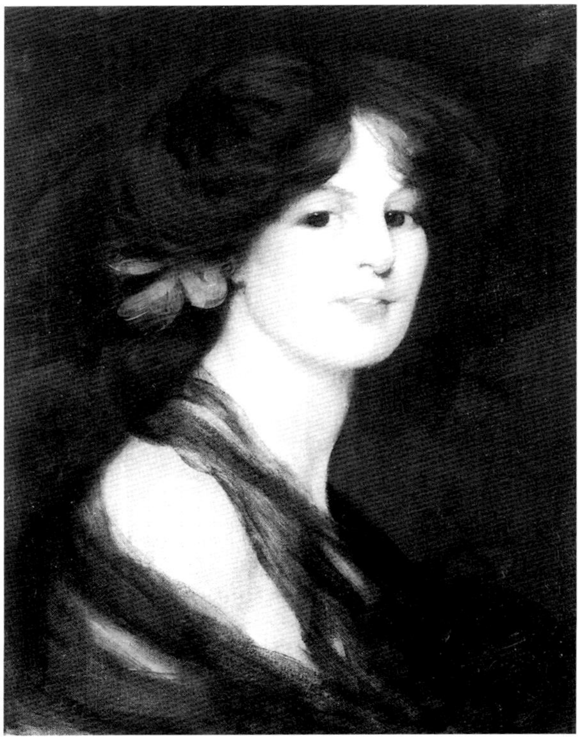

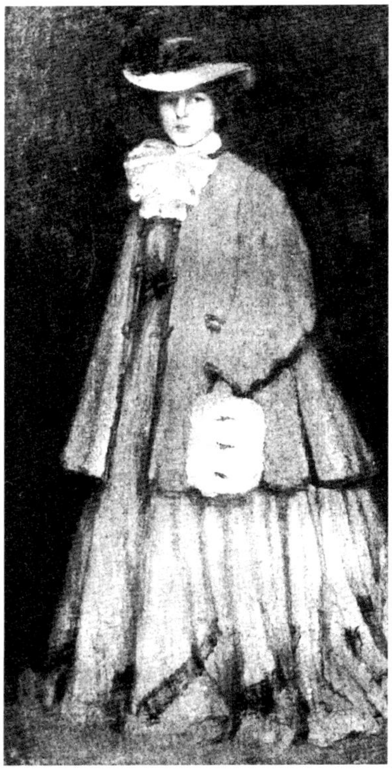

(left)
PLATE 54
'Mary'
Oil on canvas
20x16
Private collection
(photo:The Fine Art Society)

(right)
PLATE 55
The Leghorn Hat
Untraced
(photo:City of Glasgow Libraries & Archives, Mitchell Library)

Vanity was first exhibited abroad in 1901 at the Glaspalast in Munich, so it must have been painted before that date. There is some confusion as to whether one or two paintings were executed. James Caw wrote in 1908 '. . . and [in] such charming nudes as *The Toilet* and *Vanity* she comes nearer her [Berthe Morisot] in spirit than any Englishwoman I can think of.'[6] Caw may have been confused by the illustration of *Vanity* in *The Artist*, which was titled *The Toilette*.[7] It is more likely that there is only one painting and that when it came back from abroad a certain amount of repainting and alteration took place. It was redated 1902 before the First Exhibition of the Glasgow Society of Artists.

THE LEGHORN HAT

There is a description of *The Leghorn Hat* (pl.55) in the review of the Society's exhibition in the *Evening Times*: '. . . Bessie McNicol sends a number of portraits, a large one of a lady in a light-brown gown, and dark grey coat being especially attractive.'[8] This painting, yet another of the missing MacNicols, may be the work illustrated in *The Artist* as 'Portrait'. There the young lady is wearing a Leghorn straw hat, but until the actual painting is found this can only be supposition.[9]

Exhibiting with the Society were a number of women artists, including Jessie M. King and Katharine Cameron. Helen Paxton Brown, Agnes Raeburn and Janet Macdonald Aitken were other women members. The men included J. Taylor Brown, R. Russell Macnee and Andrew Law. E.A.Walton, the only Glasgow Boy to exhibit, sent a work from London, where he was living at the time.

1 *Glasgow Herald* 20 August 1928
2 *Glasgow Evening Times* 4 May 1905
3 *The Bailie* 5 March 1902 p.11
4 *Glasgow Herald* 4 April 1902
5 *The Bailie* 23 April 1902 p.10
6 Sir James Caw, *Scottish Painting 1620-1908* 1908 p.437
7 *The Artist* May 1902 p.158
8 *Glasgow Evening Times* 3 April 1902
9 *The Artist* May 1902 p.157

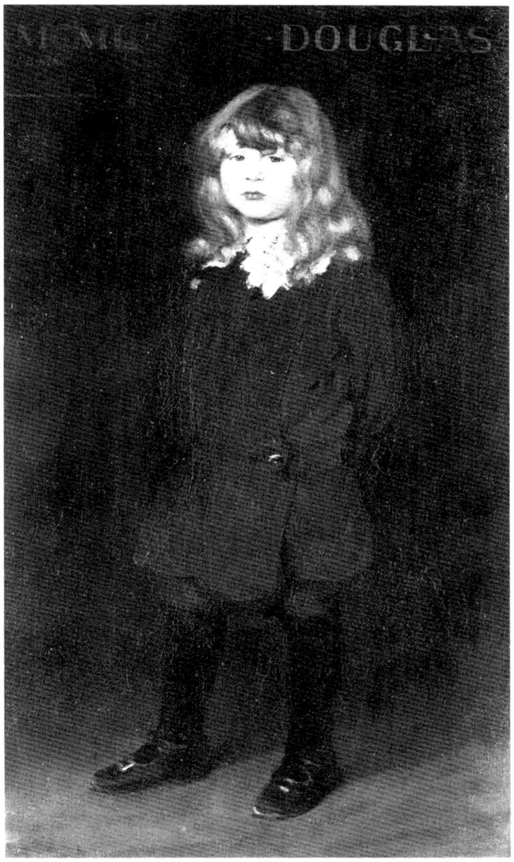

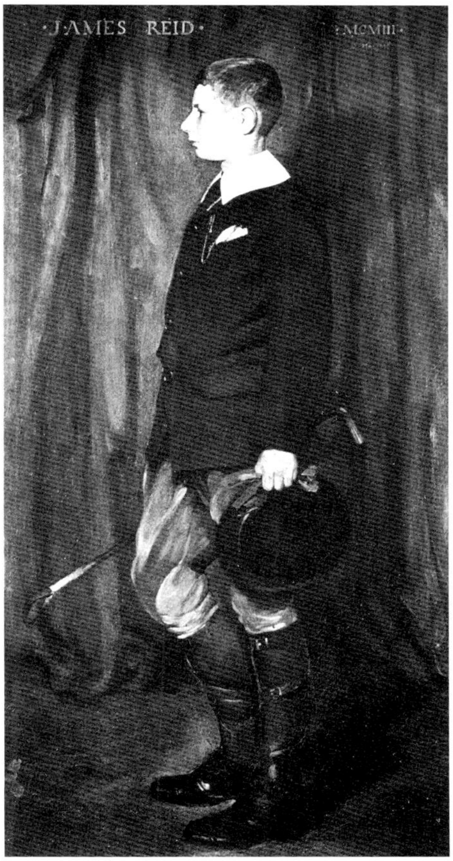

(left)
PLATE 56
Master Douglas Reid
Oil on canvas
48x28
Private collection
(photo:Sotheby's)

(right)
PLATE 57
James Reid
Untraced
(photo:City of Glasgow Libraries & Archives, Mitchell Library)

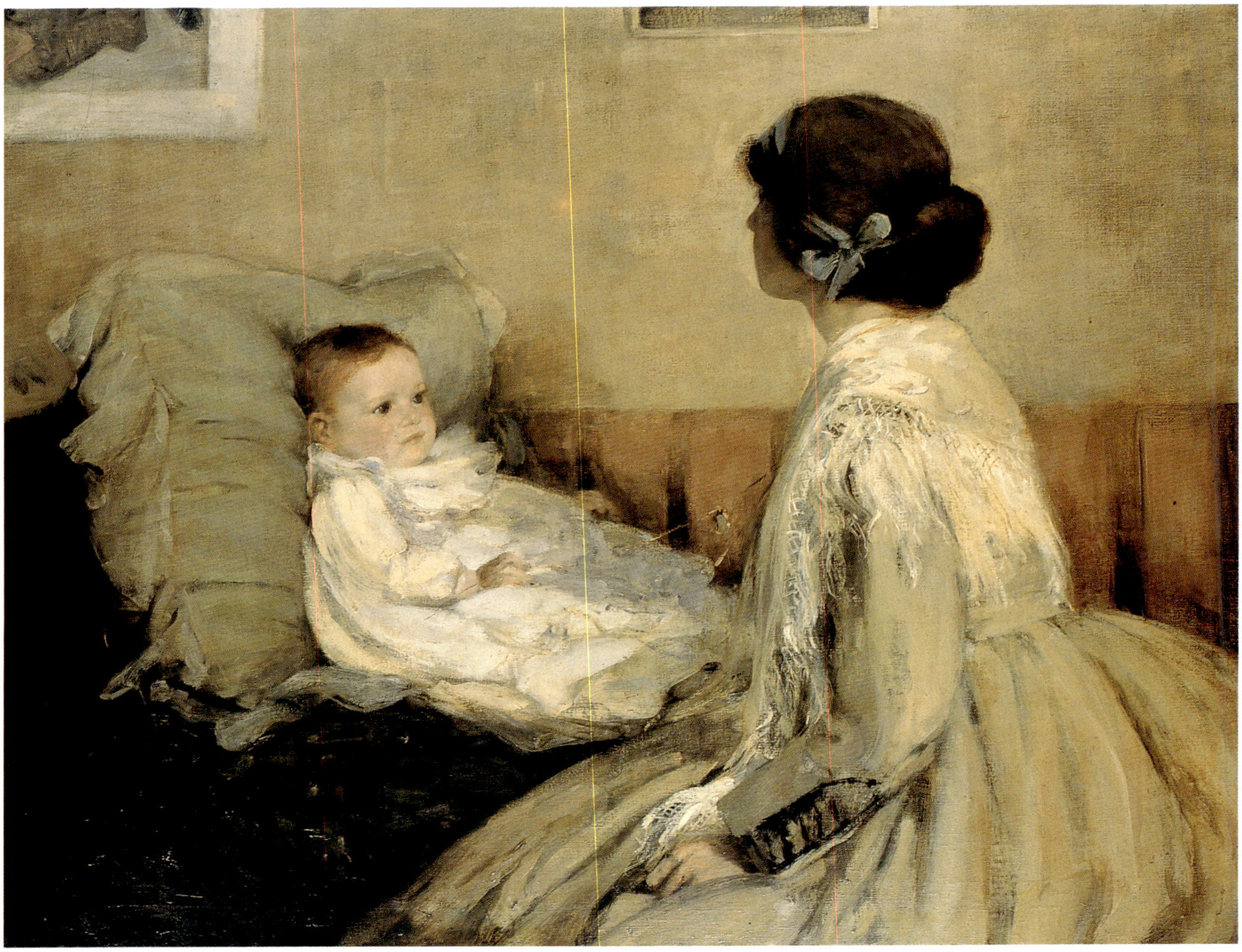

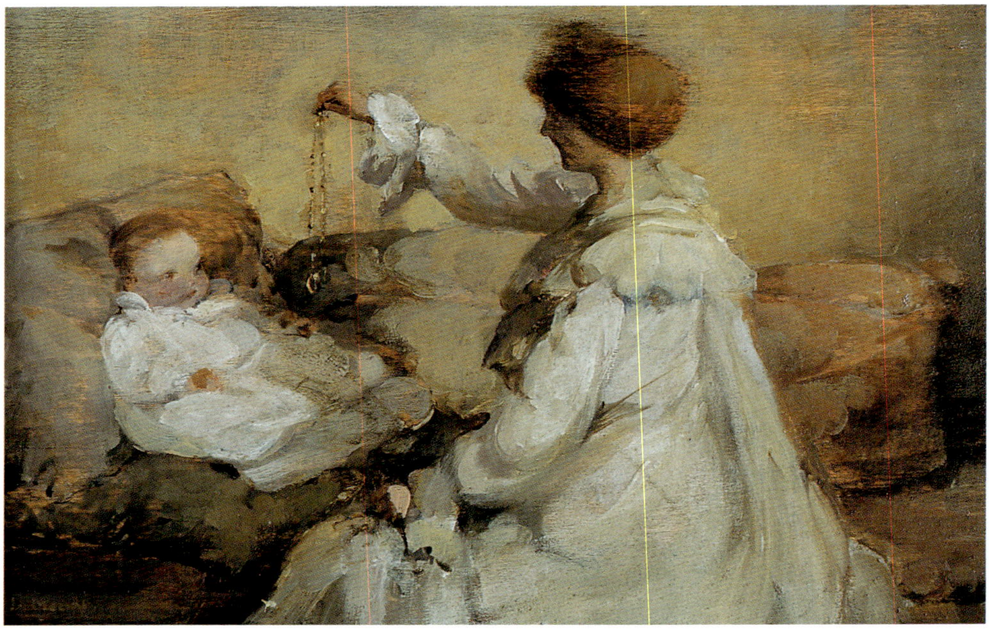

(above)
PLATE 58
Motherhood
Oil on canvas
39x50
Private collection
(photo:Sotheby's)

(left)
PLATE 59
Study for 'Motherhood'
Oil on canvas
21½x34
Private collection
(photo:R.M.Muirhead)

14. 1903

Neither Alexander Frew and Bessie MacNicol nor Jessie M. King and four other members of the Glasgow Society of Artists chose to exhibit at the Glasgow Institute in 1903. We do not know if this was an expression of protest; if it was, it lasted for only one year. However all of them exhibited at the Second Exhibition of the Society in the New Century Art Gallery at 139 Sauchiehall Street during March 1903. The President of the Society was then John Hassall, the well known poster artist; Jessie M. King was on the Council. She designed the attractive cover of the exhibition catalogue, a decorative line drawing of a young girl at a picture exhibition with a Whistlerian butterfly motif in one corner (pl.50).

MOTHERHOOD

Bessie MacNicol exhibited seven paintings, of which the most important was *Motherhood* (pl.58). Of the other six, we now know for certain only the portrait of Master Douglas Reid. *Motherhood* had been exhibited in Munich at the Glaspalast in June 1902, but this was the first time it had been shown in Glasgow. It portrays her younger sister Minnie Phoebe Alexander with her first child George, born on 18th January 1902. Most probably Bessie MacNicol saw the painting by William Quiller Orchardson *Master Baby*, which was lent to the Glasgow International Exhibition in 1901 by Mrs. Orchardson. Orchardson painted his own youngest son Gordon lying on a couch while his mother amused him with a Japanese fan. In reality Gordon was not amused by the fan for more than a few minutes and Orchardson had to use a Japanese doll as lay model.

Bessie MacNicol painted a small study (pl.59) still in the artist's family, which shows Minnie holding up a necklace in front of her son, who is propped up against a large cushion. She may have seen an illustration in *The Artist* of a painting by Philip Wilson Steer called *Hydrangeas*, now in the Fitzwilliam Museum, Cambridge, in which a young woman in the same position is holding a necklace, while playing with a kitten.[1] Much has been changed in the large painting of *Motherhood.* Now mother and baby gaze at each other. There is no outstretched arm, but the tangible link between the two is a long gold chain worn by Minnie and held by young George. Minnie is dressed in a wide-skirted crinoline and round her shoulders is a cream silk shawl. The colour is more subdued and Whistlerian than in previous paintings. It is rather low-key and subtle for such a subject, but the low tones help to bring out the white garments of the baby. Another Whistler touch is the placing of two pictures at the top of the canvas. Whistler's portrait of Carlyle had been purchased by Glasgow Corporation in 1891 and the shapes of two paintings play an important part in its composition. Is it wishful thinking or do we see at the top left corner the foot of Hornel's painting *Kite-flying, Japan* in the ivory cream frame that Bessie MacNicol preferred to a black one?

MASTER DOUGLAS REID

Master Douglas Reid (pl.56) was placed in the centre of the main wall of the Fine Art Institute. This is a portrait of the middle son of Hugh Reid DL, later Sir Hugh Reid of Tullich and Auchterarder. He is dressed in a dark green velvet knickerbocker suit with a 'Little Lord Fauntleroy' lace collar in the fashion of the day. The same year Bessie MacNicol had also painted his elder brother James as a young sportsman with a gun.[2] (pl.57) Both paintings look back to the Spanish Court and the paintings of Velasquez with their dark backgrounds and their neat inscriptions of names and dates. The portrait of James has echoes of *Philip IV as a Hunter* by Velasquez. The two portraits are obviously commissions, which Bessie MacNicol may or may not have enjoyed painting. In both one has the feeling that a conscious effort has been made to provide family heirlooms, so it is very sad to notice *Master Douglas Reid* in an auction sale in 1981. Douglas Reid became the second Baronet, when James was killed in France in 1915, while serving with the 10th Battalion Highland Light Infantry. The portrait of James has not been traced.

FAMILY MISFORTUNES

Motherhood was painted and exhibited in Germany and Glasgow before Bessie MacNicol realised that she herself was pregnant. That must have been sometime in the autumn of 1903, but it was not to be a happy year for her. On 6th May her father had died and in October her parent's home at 4 Oakfield Terrace had to be sold.

Bessie MacNicol herself never enjoyed very robust health. We learn from her letters to Hornel that she was a martyr to hay fever. In 1897 she was suffering from a liver problem of long standing, for which she had been prescribed mercury. There may have been complications in her pregnancy about which we have no knowledge. Certainly one would have thought that she was in very good hands, her husband being a leading consultant in gynaecology and obstetrics in Glasgow. There is nothing to suggest that she ever stopped painting at this time, although she must have had added responsibilities when her mother came to stay at 12 St. James Terrace, following the death of her husband. Sadly Mary Ann MacNicol died on 5th December 1903, only seven months after her husband.

1 *The Artist* February 1902
2 Percy Bate, *Modern Scottish Portrait Painters* 1910

15. 1904

Despite the sad events of the previous year Bessie MacNicol sent three works to the Institute exhibition in 1904, which was now held in the McLellan Galleries in Sauchiehall Street, as the Institute had sold their own building, the Fine Art Institute, to department store Pettigrew and Stephens. The style of *The Ermine Muff*, *'Mary'* and a watercolour *Gossips* is very different from her previous work. In the oil paintings very dark backgrounds are used as in her early self-portrait and the pigment is put on more thinly than before. Gone is the thick impasto and the bright palette of Kirkcudbright days. However what strikes one more forcibly is the appearance of a new model with dark hair and very large dark eyes, who is to be seen in almost all her later works. A full-length painting in Glasgow Art Gallery titled *Deborah* may be the only clue we have to her identity. The same very large, very dark eyes can be seen in the early *en plein air* portraits of David Gauld.

'Mary'

The large dark eyes, neat nose and shapely lips of Bessie MacNicol's model are seen in the mysteriously titled *'Mary'* (pl.54); the inverted commas in the title invite question. The placing of the head on the canvas is similar to her own self-portrait painted many years before. It leads one to think that this may be a fancy portrait of her twin sister Mary, who died when she was six years old, imagined as a grown woman.

The Ermine Muff

The Ermine Muff (pl.60) is altogether much tighter in style and execution than Bessie MacNicol's previous work. This was seen by contemporary critics as an advance in her development. Though we can admire her technical skill, it seems to lack a great deal of the spontaneous character of her earlier painting. Above all it is the large dark eyes, which seem so unnaturally enlarged and so dead, that trouble the viewer. It is almost as though belladonna drops had been administered to enlarge her pupils. *Lady with a Fan* (pl.61), another painting dated 1904, is certainly more vivacious; the model is smiling, but it is rather an enigmatic 'Mona Lisa' smile.

Phyllis in Town

In the National Galleries of Scotland is another painting of this model. *Phyllis in Town* belonged at one time to Sir Hugh Reid and then Sir John Richmond. In 1979 it was presented to the National Galleries by the latter's

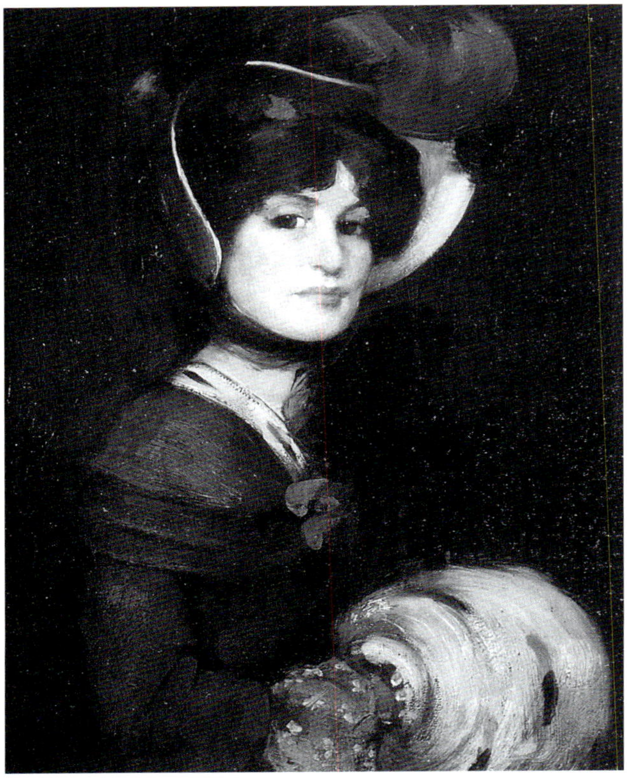

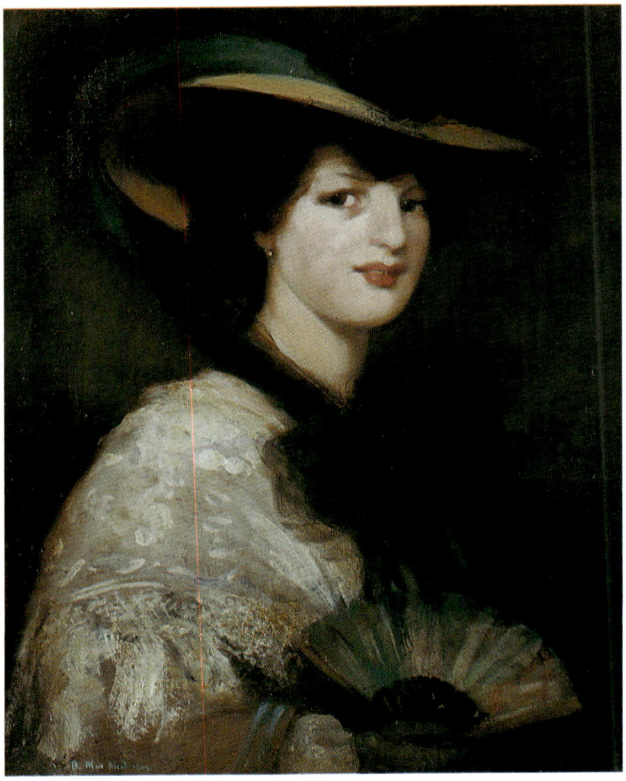

niece Mrs Isobel Traill in memory of her uncle. It is a very sweet painting of the dark haired model wearing a straw hat tied down with veiling. Associated with this painting must be a very small panel now misleadingly called *The Lace Bonnet* (pl.62), as the bonnet is not of lace, though it is trimmed with a gauze material. This may have been the first study for *Phyllis in Town.* It is a truly delightful little painting, rich in colour and executed with great spirit.

(above left)
PLATE 60
The Ermine Muff
Oil on panel
16x12
Private collection
(photo:Christie's)

(above right)
PLATE 61
Lady with a Fan
Oil on panel
14¼x10½
Private collection
(photo:Sotheby's)

Gossips

A watercolour called *Gossips* was also exhibited at the Institute Exhibition of 1904, and there are at least two other small paintings with the same title. One of these can be identified from a description by Percy Bate as a small painting showing two ladies walking in parkland with a peacock in front of them.[1] Another is on panel (pl.3) and depicts two crinolined ladies and an antique chair. This panel is similar in style to the watercolours that Bessie MacNicol had been painting for some years. The chair in the painting can also be seen in *Three Ladies of Fashion*, a watercolour dated 1903 in the National Galleries of Scotland, portraying three women, two of them in elaborate crinoline dresses. The panel belonged at one time to Sir Hugh Reid, when it may have been titled *The Arrival.* As a title *Gossips* may also have been used for a painting of two women at a tea table, which before its sale at Christie's in 1984 was in the Barogil Keith Collection and known as *The Tea Party* (pl.63).

PLATE 62
The Lace Bonnet
Oil on panel
8¾x6
Private collection
(photo:Richard Green)

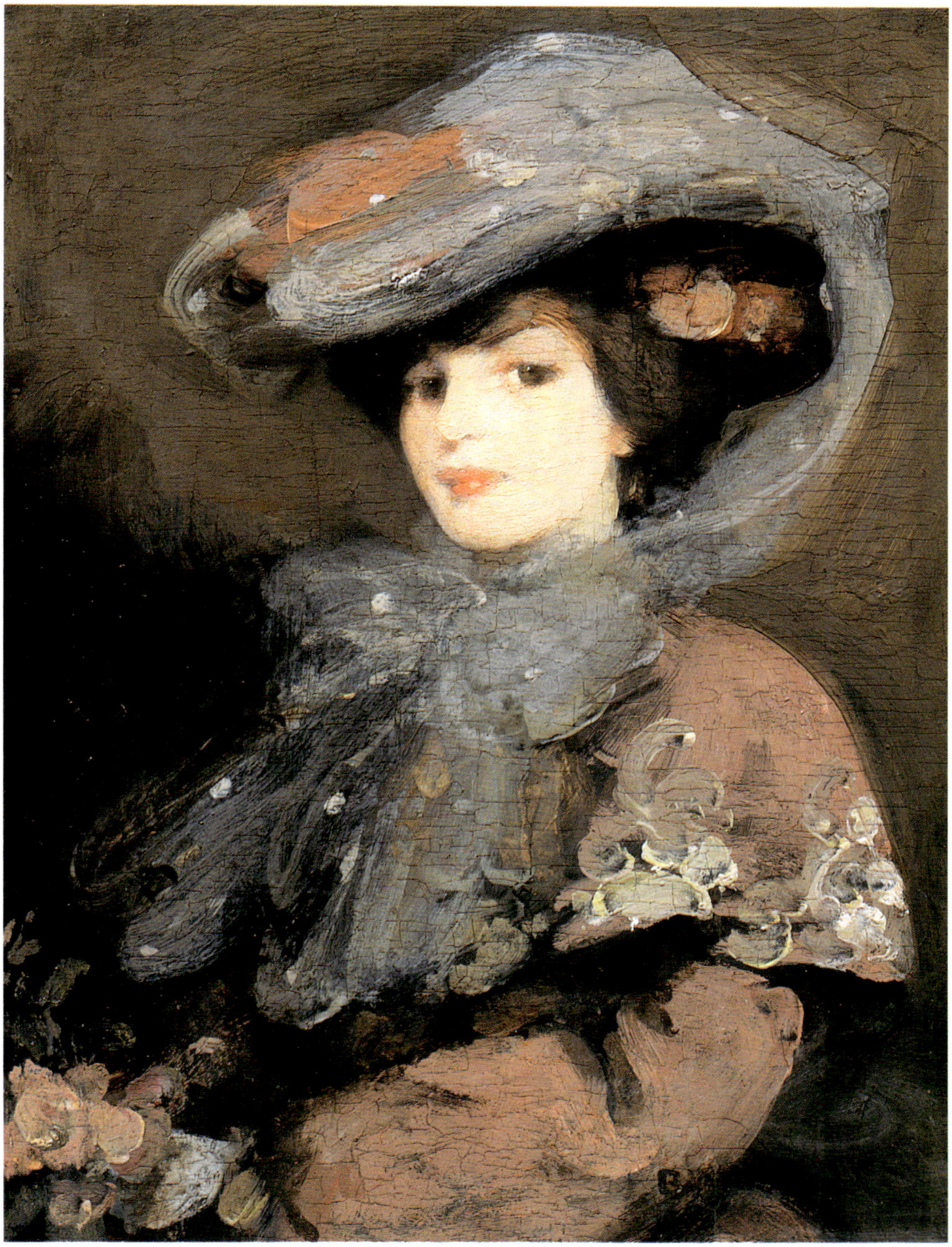

DEBORAH

The dark-haired model is seen again in the large, full-length painting called *Deborah* (pl.64), now in Glasgow Art Gallery. She is dressed in a long gown, her straw hat fastened round her neck with a veil, as if in preparation for motoring in an open car. She stands at an angle to the picture plane, her arms akimbo as she contemplates the viewer. Did Bessie MacNicol see the illustration of an oil painting titled *Au Café-Concert* by Théophile-Alexandre Steinlen, which was reproduced in *The Studio* in 1900?[2] (pl.65) The pose is very reminiscent of *Deborah*.

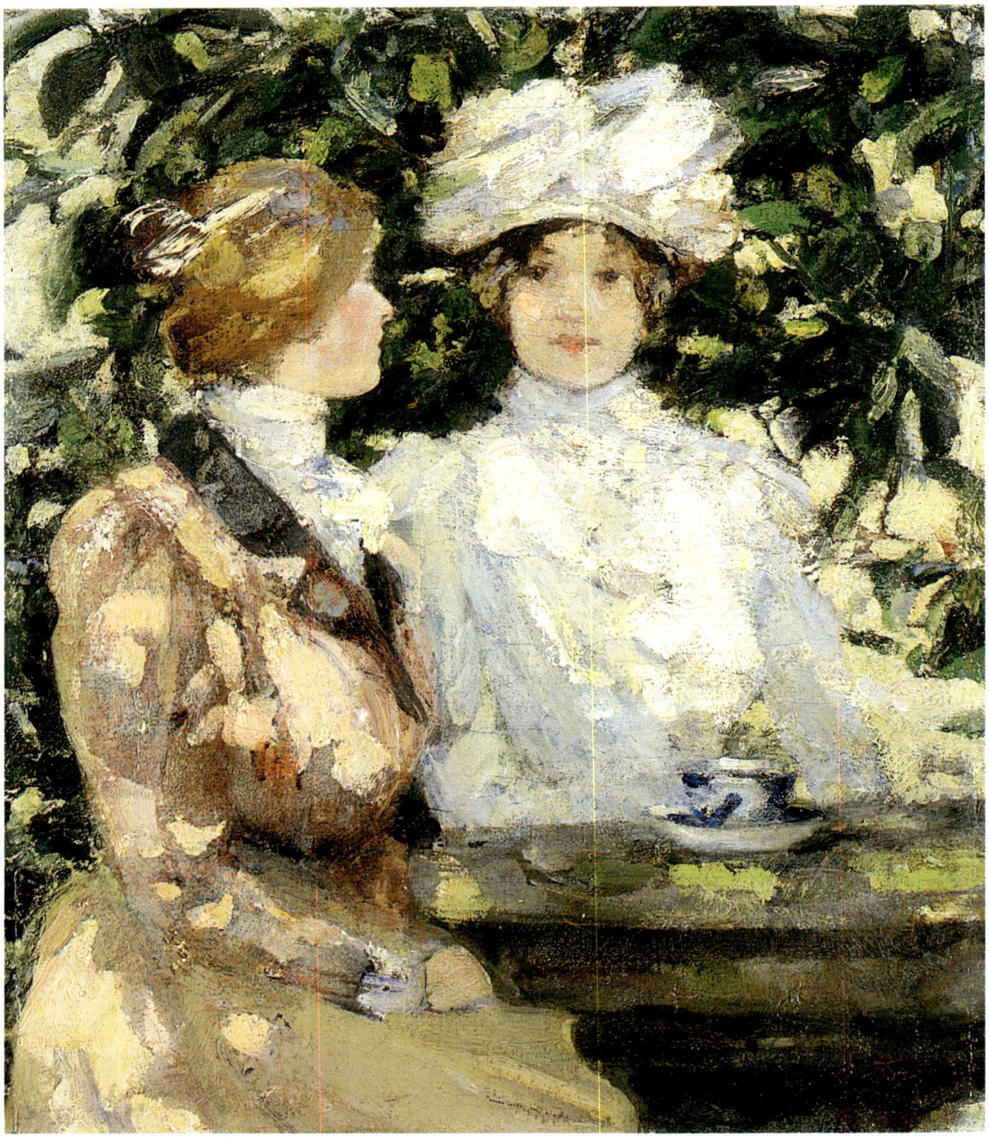

PLATE 63
The Tea Party
Oil on canvas
21x17
Private collection
(photo:Richard Green)

This may have been the last picture painted by Bessie MacNicol. Somehow it is the least satisfactory of the large works painted in the studio at 12 St. James Terrace. It may be that this model had less individuality and character in her face than Bessie MacNicol's family and friends, who had posed for her before. However there is now a slickness of technique, which replaces the sensitive, instinctive touch she had shown previously in her oil paintings, and a certain hardness is present. Of course a change in present day attitudes and taste must also be taken into account; many contemporary critics praised this picture in their reviews.

It is unfortunate that Bessie MacNicol is not represented in Glasgow Art Gallery by her other large painting *Motherhood*, as had been suggested by her friend Percy Bate. However her sister Mrs Minnie Alexander did not wish to

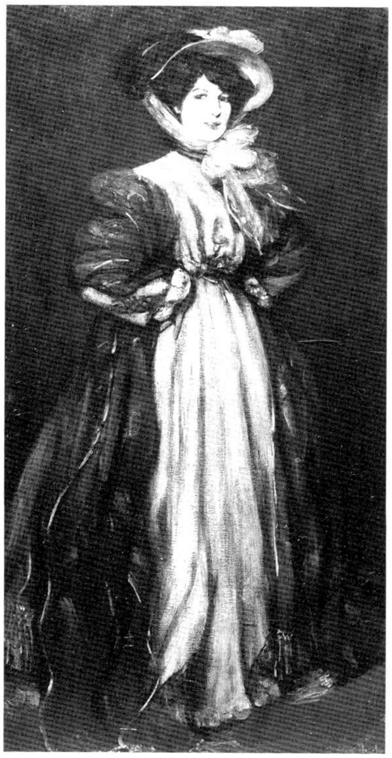

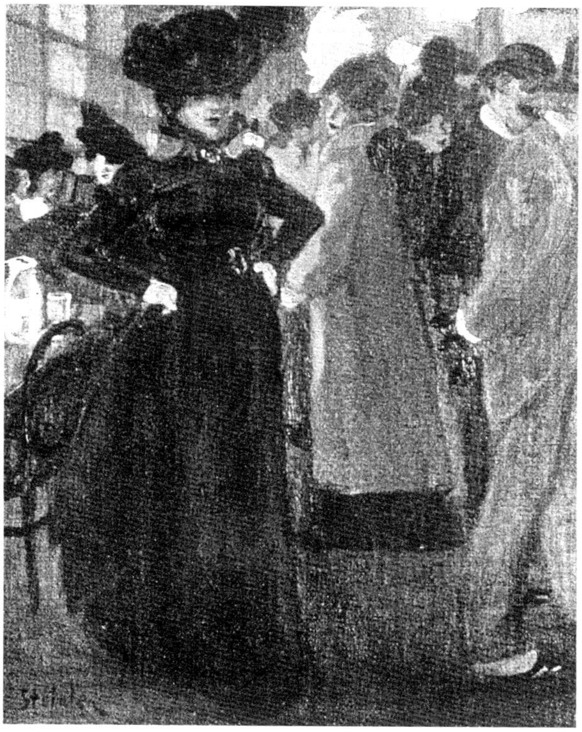

(left)
PLATE 64
Deborah
Oil on canvas
59½x35½
Glasgow Museums:
Art Gallery &
Museum, Kelvingrove

(right)
PLATE 65
THÉOPHILE-ALEXANDRE STEINLEN
Au Café-Concert
(photo:City of Glasgow Libraries & Archives, Mitchell Library)

part with the painting, quite understandably, and refused an offer of £150 from Glasgow Corporation in 1905.[3]

GLASGOW SOCIETY OF ARTISTS THIRD EXHIBITION

The third exhibition of the Society was held in the New Century Gallery, 139 Sauchiehall Street from 15th February to 12th March 1904. No catalogue has survived, so that only the works noted in reviews are known. Bessie MacNicol's full-length portrait of *Deborah* was exhibited along with *Margaret* and a smaller picture *The Bouquet* (probably a water-colour). *Margaret* is a portrait of her sister-in-law Margaret Frew, who married Dr. Ewing Hunter of Helensburgh in 1898. (pl.66)

WHOM THE GODS LOVE DIES YOUNG

The Frews' child was never born. At 8 pm on 4th June 1904 Bessie MacNicol died. The cause of death was given as 'Puerperal Eclampsia before labour' and the death certificate was signed by Alexander Frew, who had been present. She was a month short of her thirty-fifth birthday.

In a collection of photographs in the possession of the artist's family one of the photographs of Bessie MacNicol has written on the back 'Bessie MacNicol married Dr. Alexander Frew, both were artists of great competence. Died aged 36 [sic] of an undiagnosed transverse presentation.' There is no way of checking this information and it cannot undo the harm that was done. Whoever was at fault, if fault there was, and for whatever reason, the tragedy had taken place. Dr. Alexander Frew's expertise was unable to save the lives of his wife and unborn child and he had to live with this for the rest of his life.

The funeral took place on 8th June at Sighthill Cemetery, Glasgow. A Glasgow newspaper reported:

> There was quite a pathetic little scene at Sighthill Cemetery this afternoon, when the remains of Mrs. Alexander Frew (Miss Bessie MacNicol) were laid to rest. Many of her brother artists went to pay their tribute to the memory of the deceased. The grave was covered with wreaths, including a large one inscribed 'From the Glasgow Art Club, with sincere regret for the loss of a true artist.'[4]

Many papers and periodicals printed glowing tributes, which acknowledged her place in European art while lamenting the premature loss of one who seemed to have much more to say in a future which was not to be hers. The critic of the *Glasgow Herald* wrote:

> So brilliant was her work and of such promise that it is felt that her premature death has robbed Scotland of one who would have left a name worthy to rank with the best of her artist sons.[5]

1 Percy Bate, op. cit. 1904, p200
2 *The Studio* vol.XIX February 1900 p58
3 Council Minutes of the Royal Glasgow Institute of the Fine Arts 18 May 1905
4 *Glasgow Evening News* 8 June 1904
5 *Glasgow Herald* 7 June 1904

16. 1905

Memorial Exhibition

In March 1905 a Memorial Exhibition was held at the galleries of Craibe Angus & Son in Glasgow, consisting of forty-five works: oil paintings, watercolours and pastels. It is a sad fact that Bessie MacNicol did not sell many of her paintings during her lifetime and at her Memorial Exhibition at least twenty-eight of the forty-five paintings remained unsold, even though much of her best work was included. This was despite most favourable reviews of the exhibition. The *Evening Times* went so far as to say '. . . Her genius was widely recognised at home and abroad and her work stamped her as one of the few women who can really be called great artists.'[1] Hopes were expressed at the end of the article that 'examples of this talented Glasgow-born and Glasgow-bred artist may be timeously secured for our civic galleries.' However that was not to be until after the death of Alexander Frew in 1908 and then it was not her best work. It was not until the bequest of John Keppie in 1945 and the purchase of *Under the Apple Tree* in 1963 that Bessie MacNicol was adequately represented in the collection of Glasgow Art Gallery.

Glasgow Society of Artists Fourth Exhibition

The fourth exhibition of the Society was held in May 1905, not in Glasgow but in London at the Doré Gallery, 35 Old Bond Street. Listed in the catalogue as by 'the late Bessie MacNicol' were five paintings – four oils and one watercolour – with *Deborah* as the centrepiece. The London Special Correspondent who supplied the review in the *Evening Times* was very complimentary:

> . . . The work of the late Miss Bessie MacNicol (Mrs. Frew) comes to one who had seen little of it for some years with a fresh shock of delight. It is difficult to speak critically of this delightful, sincere, and individual painter, whose death was a loss to European art. Like Charles Furse, she was a born painter, who lived only long enough for us to know something of what we had lost, and to leave no successor. . . . A graceful, impetuous girlhood seems to linger in all this lady painted. She takes her place with Mme. Morisot among the few original women painters of the past century.[2]

Glasgow Society of Artists Last Exhibitions

Two works by Bessie MacNicol were shown in the Sixth Exhibition held in February 1908. These were *Deborah* and *Vanity*, which must have been unsold at the Sale of Paintings by Alexander Frew and Bessie MacNicol held by Robert McTear & Co the previous day.

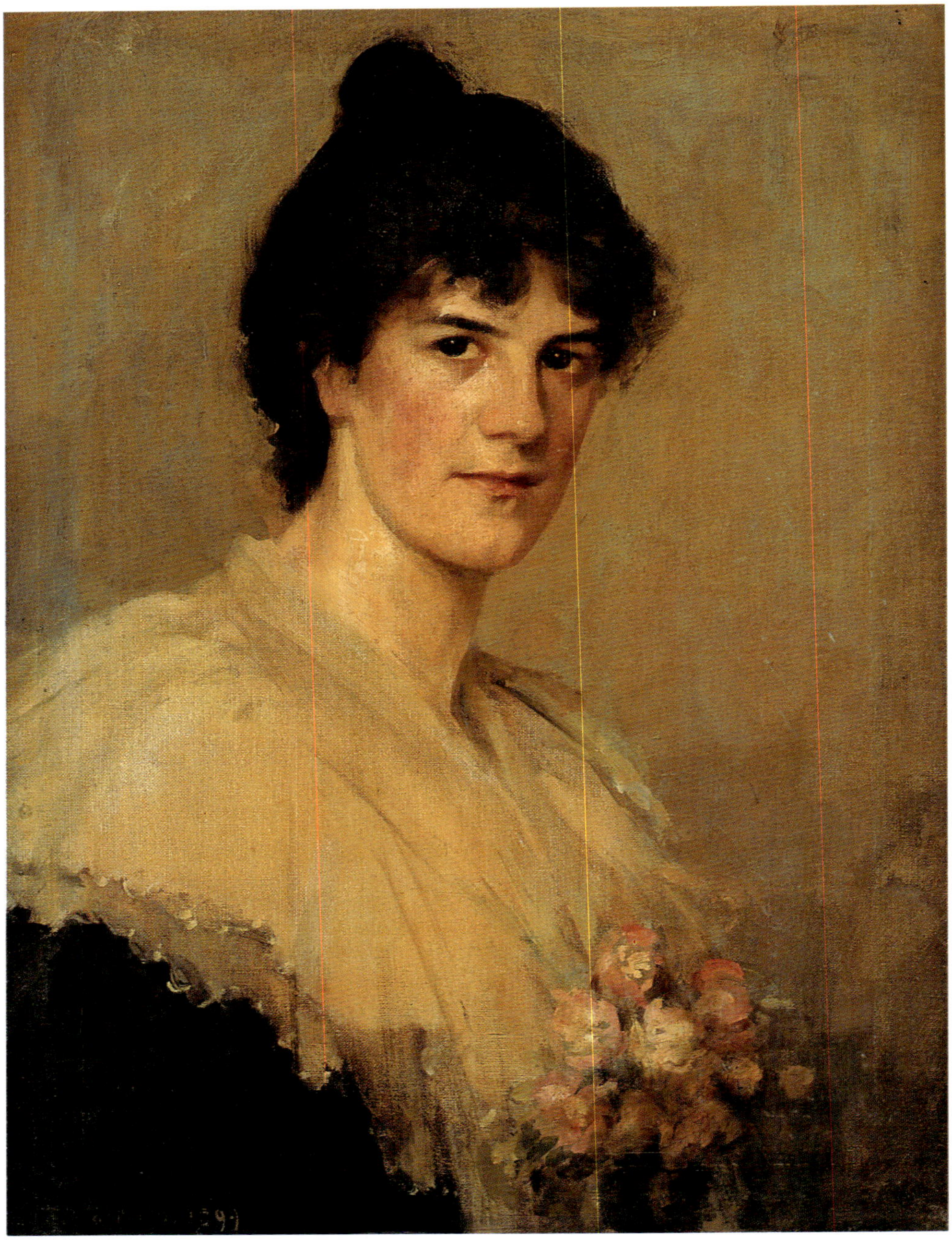

PLATE 66
Margaret Ewing Hunter
Oil on canvas
24x18
Private collection
(photo:R.M.Muirhead)

John Hassall had been President of the Glasgow Society of Artists from the Second Exhibition and continued in office until the Seventh Exhibition in the Glasgow Institute Galleries in October 1909, which was probably the last held by the Society. This was a large exhibition of 130 works, but there were few by major artists. Women had always been encouraged to exhibit and on this occasion there were works by Jessie M. King and Agnes Raeburn, both founder members, and Annie Urquhart.

Alexander Frew

Frew continued to live at 12 St. James Terrace in the years following his wife's death and found some relief in conchology and in forming a collection of molluscs, which he presented to the Hunterian Museum in 1907. The same year he remarried, his bride being a young singer Olive Jenevera Jarvis, who sang as a contralto under her professional name of Olive Tree. The marriage took place on 7th June at 12 St. James Terrace. His friend Revd William Jeffrey, who had taken the service on his marriage to Bessie MacNicol, officiated once again and the minister's wife Margaret and John Rennie were witnesses. Olive Jarvis was twenty-one and Frew forty-four. Her home was in Brighton, but little is known about her. It was hoped by Frew's friends that he would regain some happiness in this new marriage, but perhaps that was not the case. Only seven months later on 12th January 1908, the day after he had attended a concert in which Olive was a soloist, Alexander Frew committed suicide. Apparently he had been in indifferent health and was subject to depression. The death certificate was not corrected by the medical attendant to include the word 'suicide' until after the funeral and burial in Sighthill Cemetery on 14th January 1908. It appears that Frew died intestate as no will has ever been found.

His widow must have arranged for Robert McTear & Co. to hold a sale of pictures by Frew and Bessie MacNicol in the Royal Exchange Sale-Rooms on 31st January 1908. A useful catalogue was printed, which included a long obituary notice from the *Evening Times* of 16th January by George Eyre-Todd titled 'A Remarkable Career'. In the sale were thirty-two paintings by Frew, forty-nine by Bessie MacNicol and a dozen works by other artists, which included a portrait of Bessie MacNicol by A.C.Holms.

After the sale of 12 St. James Terrace, Olive Frew went to live at 37 Cranworth Street, Glasgow, where she must have met George James Campbell, a railway contractor on leave from India living at the same address. In the *Glasgow Herald* of 7th December 1908 the following announcement appeared:

> CAMPBELL - TREE
> On 4th December, George James Campbell of Treesbank, Ayrshire to Olive Tree. (Indian papers please copy)

It has not been possible to trace what became of Olive Jenevera Frew or Campbell. Perhaps she went out to India and may have died there. Campbell came back to this country as an invalid and died in Surbiton on 18th August 1937. His will does not mention a wife or that he was a widower. His estate of Treesbank, Riccarton near Kilmarnock had been sold in 1919.

1 *Evening Times* 15 March 1905
2 *Evening Times* 4 May 1905

17. EPILOGUE

Various scraps of information have been gathered and assembled and, like little gleams of light on a dark night, they tell us tantalizingly little of the woman and artist who was Bessie MacNicol. Her own letters, so few but so vivid, do help to lessen the gloom for a short while, but make the returning night seem darker.

What we do have today are some, but by no means all, of her paintings in oil and watercolour, together with a few pastels. They can speak to us more directly with their verve and vitality, demonstrating her love of colour and her interest in paint and what she could do with it.

Many are intimate communications concerning young girls and nature. In these paintings the sun shines through foliage on to their faces and dresses. Is it too fanciful to imagine that her women are emerging into light and freedom from the conventions of the Victorian era? Bessie and her sisters were representatives of 'New Woman' at that time in Glasgow.

Bessie MacNicol also painted portraits of men and had to pay for her own unconventional behaviour in painting Hornel in his own studio. Her portrait of him and of Alexander Frew and his friends are objective professional statements, but these were sufficiently unusual at that time to confuse critical reaction. To this day her rightful place alongside the younger Glasgow Boys is not fully appreciated. No elaborate claims are being made of her as a leader, but recognition should be given to her as comrade and fellow artist.

True her career was cut short and we do not know how her work would have developed. Her later works, though brilliantly painted, are enigmatic. They lack the freshness and vitality and also the depth of her earlier work, appearing somewhat slick and mannered. It may be that, even had she lived longer, her earlier work, like that of some of the Glasgow Boys, would still have been her best.

Contemporary criticism of her day, though at times misdirected and prejudiced, was kinder to Bessie MacNicol than history. Her name could very easily have slipped away into oblivion and her work in public collections could have lain unseen in storerooms. It must be thanks in some measure to the commercial art galleries and to the private collector that her work continues to be appreciated. Her quality as a painter is obvious and will be recognised as long as there are people with eyes to see beyond current trends and prejudices, for Bessie MacNicol had above all, as Percy Bate rightly observed, the gift of paint.[1]

1 Percy Bate, op.cit. 1904 p.198

SELECTED BIBLIOGRAPHY

DICTIONARIES

Peter J.M.McEwan, *Dictionary of Scottish Art & Architecture*, Woodbridge 1994
Delia Gaze (ed), *Dictionary of Women Artists* (2 vols.), London 1997
Paul Harris & Julian Halsby, *The Dictionary of Scottish Painters 1600-1960*, Edinburgh 1990
Macmillan, *The Dictionary of Art* (34 vols.), London 1997

BOOKS

Percy Bate, *Modern Scottish Portrait Painters*, Edinburgh 1910
Roger Billcliffe, *The Glasgow Boys: The Glasgow School of Painting 1875-1895*, London 1985
Jude Burkhauser (ed), *Glasgow Girls: Women in the Art School 1880-1920*, Glasgow 1988
Jude Burkhauser (ed), *Glasgow Girls: Women in Art and Design 1880-1920*, Edinburgh 1990
Sir James L.Caw, *Scottish Painting, Past and Present 1620-1908*, Edinburgh 1908
Sir James L.Caw, *Sir James Guthrie*, London 1932
Elizabeth Cumming (ed), *Glasgow 1900: Art and Design*, Amsterdam 1993
Hugh Ferguson, *Glasgow School of Art: The History*, Glasgow 1995
William Hardie, *Scottish Painting: 1837 to the Present*, London 1990
Janice Helland, *The Studios of Frances and Margaret Macdonald*, Manchester 1996
Perilla Kinchin & Juliet Kinchin, *Glasgow's Great Exhibitions*, Bicester 1960
Duncan Macmillan, *Scottish Art 1460-1990*, Edinburgh 1990
Duncan Macmillan, *Scottish Art in the 20th Century*, Edinburgh 1994
Neil Munro, *The Brave Days*, Edinburgh 1931
Bill Smith, *D.Y.Cameron: The Visions of the Hills*, Edinburgh 1992
Bill Smith, *Hornel: The Life & Work of Edward Atkinson Hornel*, Edinburgh 1997
Colin White, *The Enchanted World of Jessie M King*, Edinburgh 1989

CATALOGUES, ARTICLES, ETC

Barbican Art Gallery, *Japan and Britain: An Aesthetic Dialogue 1850-1930*, London 1991
Chapman 27-28 vol.VI no.1, Ailsa Tanner, *Some Scottish Women Artists of the Past*, 1980
Irene Doris, Thesis on Bessie MacNicol for Open University, 1992
Evening Times 16 Jan.1908, George Eyre-Todd, *A Remarkable Career: The Late Dr. Alexander Frew*
The Fine Art Society, *Glasgow School of Painting*, catalogue by William Hardie, London 1970
Glasgow Herald 16 Feb.1974, John Weyers, *Woman whose art still blossoms in obscurity*
Glasgow Society of Women Artists, *A Centenary Exhibition to celebrate the Founding of the Glasgow Society of Lady Artists in 1882*, catalogue by Ailsa Tanner, Glasgow 1982
Helensburgh & District Art Club, *West of Scotland Women Artists*, catalogue by Ailsa Tanner, 1976
Hunterian Art Gallery, *Margaret Macdonald Mackintosh 1864-1933*, catalogue by Pamela Robertson
Lillie Art Gallery, *Stansmore Dean Stevenson 1866-1944*, catalogue by Ailsa Tanner, Milngavie 1984
Scots Magazine cxxxiv Nov.1990, Ailsa Tanner, *Portrait of a Portrait*
Scottish Art and Letters vol.III no.3, Percy Bate, *In Memoriam: Bessie MacNicol, Painter*, 1904
The Scottish Arts Council, *The Glasgow Boys* (2 parts), Edinburgh 1968 & 1971

LETTERS

Letters from Bessie MacNicol to E.A.Hornel, December 1896 - December 1897, The National Trust for Scotland, Broughton House, Kirkcudbright

WORKS EXHIBITED

Royal Glasgow Institute of the Fine Arts

1893	161	Study of a Head	NFS
1894	55	St Monance	£10.10
	492	Phoebe	£15.15
1895	47	A French Girl	£20.00
	444	Summer	£25.00
1896	411	Head of a Girl	£20.00
	416	Portrait	NFS
1897	456	E. A. Hornel	NFS
	639	A Dutch Girl	£40.00
1898	589	Under the Apple Tree	£35.00
1899	292	The Goose Girl	£50.00
1900	79	Portrait (Alexander Frew)	NFS
	404	A Girl of the Sixties	£35.00
1901	44	Portrait (John Rennie)	NFS
	482	Portrait (a man)	NFS
1901*	18	Portrait (a lady)	NFS
1901*	69	At the Dressmaker	£12.00
	96	Tritomas	£35.00
	132	The Butterfly Pinafore	£15.00
1902	41	Baby (Baby Crawford)	NFS
	205	Mr Edgar Barratt	NFS
1904	133	The Ermine Muff	£15.15
	611	Gossips (watercolour)	£10.10
	766	'Mary'	£40.00

The late Bessie MacNicol

1905	73	In the Orchard (lent by Hugh Hopkins)
	155	Portrait (lent by Hugh Reid)
	177	Motherhood
1935	110	A French Girl (lent by Hugh Hopkins)
1941	2	Interior (lent by J.Arnold Fleming)

*Autumn Exhibition

Glasgow Society of Artists

1902	4	Vanity	£80.00
	9	A Japanese Robe	£20.00
	14	Lamplight	£30.00
	18	The Leghorn Hat	£70.00
	21	Japanese Embroidery	£40.00
	46	Midsummer	£15.00
	54	Winter	£6.00
	56	In the Wood	£15.00
	61	Girl in Green	£20.00
	66	Portrait	NFS
	74	Sketch	£3.00
	76	A Visitor	£10.00
	78	Sketch	£3.00
	109	The Curtsey	£6.00
	111	At the Dressmakers	£10.00
	113	Debutante	£6.00
1902	114	A Wallflower	£6.00
1903	16	Queen of the May	
	18	Portrait	
	30	Master Douglas Reid	
	37	A Coquette	
	45	Motherhood	
	85	Sweet Seventeen	
	93	Entrée du Bal	

The late Bessie MacNicol

1905	1	Under the Apple Tree	£70.00
	11	Lamplight	£70.00
	12	Baby	£50.00
	16	Deborah	£200.00
	36	Apple Blossom	£50.00
	42	At Home	£25.00

Glasgow International Exhibition 1901

431 Apple Blossom (lent by the artist)

Royal Scottish Academy

1897	251	Emily	£20.00
1899	115	A Haymaker	£25.00
	615	A Wallflower	£6.00
1901	161	Tritomas	£40.00
	320	Confidences	£40.00

Royal Scottish Society of Painters in Water-colours

1898	54	A Portrait Study

London, Royal Academy

1893	326	Fifeshire Interior

London, International Society of Sculptors, Painters and Gravers

1898	57	Autumn
	121	Children
	133	La Débutante
	156	Blind Man's Buff
	170	The Emboidery
1899	D80	Her First Ball (watercolour)
	110	Under the Apple Tree
1901	1	A Girl of the Sixties
1904	177	Vanity

London, Clifford Gallery 1901

(Glasgow paintings intended for the Royal Academy and delayed in transit)

3	A Haymaker	£25.00
13	In the Wood	£15.00
18	At the Dressmakers	£20.00
40	Lamplight	£50.00
46	Entrée du Bal	£12.00
55	The Curtsey	£12.00
59	The Green Parasol	£10.00

London, Whitechapel Art Gallery

1912	114	Herself (lent by John Keppie)

London, Earl's Court: Women's Exhibition 1900

The Goose Girl

London, Grafton Galleries: Women's International Art Club Exhibition 1910

Motherhood
Vanity

Liverpool, Walker Art Gallery Autumn Exhibition

1898	1063	A Daughter of Firenze	£30.00
1899	1107	Under the Apple Tree	
1902	1007	Lamplight	£50.00
1905	1141	Vanity	£50.00

Manchester, Manchester Academy of Fine Arts Autumn Exhibition

1899	203	A Dutch Girl	£35.00
	221	Tritomas	£40.00
	223	Midsummer	£25.00

Munich, Glaspalast

1895	435a	A Dutch Girl
	435b	Phoebe
1897	1067	Blind Man's Buff
1901	1107	Vanity
1903	742	Motherhood
	743	A Girl of the Sixties

Munich, 'Secession' Internationale Kunst Ausstellung 1896

	248	Mädchenkopf
	249	Ein schottisches Mädchen

Ghent

1899	46	Lady in Green
	787	Study

Vienna, Secession Kunstausstellung der Vereinigung Bildener Künstler Österreichs

1898	13a	Tritomas
1910	93	Self Portrait

Venice Fine Art Exhibition

1899	31	Lamplight
	32	A Battle of Flowers

Düsseldorf, Internationalen Kunstausstellung im Stadtischen Kunstpalast

1904	1023	Vanity (Eitelkeit)

St Louis Exposition and Music Hall Association

1896	328	Evening
	329	Lamplight
1896	330	A Parisienne
1897	325	Rose

Pittsburgh, Carnegie Institute Annual Exhibition

1897	164	A Dutch Girl
1898		Under the Apple Tree
1899	166	Under the Greenwood Tree
1900	171	Midsummer
1901	148	Causerie

Memorial Exhibition
at the galleries of Craibe Angus & Son, 106 Hope Street, Glasgow, March 1905

Oils

1	Vanity	13	The Butterfly Frock	25	The Leghorn Hat
2	Deborah	14	A Haymaker	26	The Boudoir
3	The Goose Girl	15	The Vicar's Daughter	27	Netta
4	Confidences	16	Galloway Landscape	28	The Blue Bow
5	Tritomas	17	The Joiner's Shop	29	Winter
6	A Girl of the Sixties	18	Midsummer	30	Hampstead
7	May Day	19	St Monan's	31	Gossips
8	Lamplight	20	A Fife Harbour	32	Ermine
9	Under the Apple Tree	21	The Lilac Sunbonnet	33	At Home
10	A Puritan	22	Old Mill, Kirkcudbright	34	The Novel
11	A Dutch Girl	23	Iona Cathedral	35	Frills and Furbelows
12	Apple Blossom	24	Phyllis in Town		

Pastels

36	Mademoiselle	37	Waiting

Watercolours

38	The Sofa	41	The Feather Fan	44	The Spanish Dancer
39	A Distinguished Visitor	42	The Blue Hat	45	The Feather Boa
40	The Bouquet	43	Grey and Sable		

Works Sold at Auction
at the Royal Exchange Salerooms of Robert McTear & Co in Glasgow on 31 January 1908

33	Old Mill, Kirkcudbright	20x20	50	Deborah	72x36	67	Lamplight	30x25
34	Iona Cathedral, Moonlight	12x16	51	A Welcome Seat	42x30	68	Tritomas	30x25
35	The Carpenter	16x24	52	The Merry Children	24x30	69	A Dutch Girl	24x20
36	A Spanish Dancer (W)	12x9	53	Apple Blossom	24x20	70	Still Life	27x19
37	The White Fan (W)	10x7	54	The Puritan	27x20	71	Galloway Landscape	20x27
38	Grey and Sable (W)	10x8	55	Mademoiselle (P)	22x16	72	Afternoon Tea	21x17
39	The Feather Boa (W)	10x8	56	Waiting (P)	22x16	73	Portrait Study	12x16
40	Netta	14x10	57	When the Heart is Young	18x14	74	The Vicar's Daughter	20x16
41	St Monans	18x14	58	Playtime	20x12	75	The Goose Girl	52x32
42	The Quay-side	14x18	59	The Novel	14x12	76	A Girl of the Sixties	32x24
43	A Fife Harbour	16x12	60	In the Woods	10x14	77	The Butterfly Frock	19x16
44	Causerie	42x30	61	At Home	8x10	78	Portrait of a Lady	16x12
45	Confidences	24x30	62	The Blue Hat (W)	12x9	79	Vanity	54x58
46	Under the Apple Tree	30x26	63	Portrait of the Artist (D)	6x4	80	The Leghorn Hat	12x9
47	Spring Time	30x18	64	Figure Subject	10x14	81	Portrait Study	14x10
48	An Afternoon Rest	24x18	65	Geraniums	12x14			
49	The Lilac Sunbonnet	19x16	66	A Baby's Portrait	24x20			

WORKS IN PUBLIC COLLECTIONS

ABERDEEN ART GALLERY

Autumn oil on canvas 24x20

NATIONAL GALLERY OF SCOTLAND, EDINBURGH

Phyllis in Town 1904 oil on panel 14x11
Three Ladies of Fashion watercolour $11\frac{3}{4}$x$10\frac{1}{4}$

THE CITY ART CENTRE, EDINBURGH

Baby Crawford 1902 oil on canvas $24\frac{1}{4}$x20
The Green Hat after 1896 oil on canvas $20\frac{1}{4}$x14

GLASGOW ART GALLERY AND MUSEUM

A Galloway Landscape c1899 oil on canvas 20x27
Portrait of the Artist 1894 oil on canvas 16x12
Under the Apple Tree 1896 & 1899 oil on canvas 29x$25\frac{1}{4}$
A Girl of the 'Sixties' c1899 oil on canvas 32x24
Deborah c1904 oil on canvas $59\frac{1}{2}$x$35\frac{1}{2}$

HUNTERIAN ART GALLERY, UNIVERSITY OF GLASGOW

Lamplight 1901 oil on canvas 30x25

FERENS ART GALLERY, HULL

Two Sisters 1897 oil on panel 11x$14\frac{1}{2}$

THE NATIONAL TRUST FOR SCOTLAND, BROUGHTON HOUSE, KIRKCUDBRIGHT

E. A. Hornel 1896 oil on canvas 30x24

PERTH MUSEUM AND ART GALLERY

Girl in Sunbonnet 1898 oil on canvas $19\frac{1}{2}$x$15\frac{1}{2}$

LIST OF PLATES